If I Die Today

If I Die Today

SHASHI DESHPANDE

RAINLIGHT

RUPA

First published in 2012
in RAINLIGHT by Rupa Publications India Pvt. Ltd.
7/16, Ansari Road, Daryaganj
New Delhi 110002

Sales centres:
Allahabad Bengaluru Chennai
Hyderabad Jaipur Kathmandu
Kolkata Mumbai

First impression 2012

ISBN: 978-81-291-2049-6

10 9 8 7 6 5 4 3 2 1

Shashi Deshpande asserts the moral right to be identified as the
author of this work.

Typeset in 10/14 pt Nebraska Roman by SÜRYA, New Delhi

Printed and bound in India by
Repro Knowledgecast Limited, Thane

'Then in good faith is there no more difference between your grace and me, but that I shall die today, and you tomorrow.'

—Sir Thomas More

Author's Note

Having lived for several years in hospital campuses, at first in Bombay and then in Bangalore, it is not surprising that I used the milieu of such a campus as the locale for one of my novels. However, since *If I Die Today* is a crime novel, it becomes important to make the usual disclaimer, that all the characters in this novel have come out of my imagination and that they have no connection with any person, living or dead. I need to emphasize this, since most of the doctors I lived among were not only good and humane doctors, but also good friends and neighbours; in fact, some of the best years of my life were lived in these campuses.

This novel began its life as a serial and was subsequently published by Vikas in 1982 in a slightly lengthier form. I have used my author's privilege to make some changes in it yet again, though in essence it remains what it originally was—a story of human frailty and human strength.

Shashi Deshpande
Bangalore

One

It's a piquant thought—if it weren't for the fact that a village doctor had once, in his benevolence, charitably looked after a poor widow and her three children, none of us would have been here. In fact, there wouldn't have been a S.D.M. Medical College and Hospital, either. For, when the widow's dogged, eldest son got his first million, one of the first things he had done had been to endow a trust in his mother's name for a medical college and hospital, which, he hoped, would be the best in the country. He didn't get very far beyond staking out a plot; but *his* son, after the father's death, took it up with the same determination that had given his father his millions. I've seen this man, the son, once or twice. Sethji, they call him. He looks a typical businessman, shrewd, portly and complacent. A man, you'd think, who has no thoughts but of making money. But his eyes, I don't know why, they remind me of Martin Luther King's words: 'I have a dream.'

Yes, maybe you've got to be a visionary to build anything: a nation, a religion, a movement, a synthetic textile business, or a hospital like ours. And our Sethji is a visionary—one who can effectively translate his vision into a reality. I can imagine him working out his dream into something real. Sitting with the architect, watching the dream take shape, on paper at first, helping the architect to do so. Jabbing a forceful finger at the sketch and saying, The hospital, here. Hostels for students, here. Houses for staff, here. He thought of everything, did the Sethji, from schools and playgrounds for the children, from parks and shops, to trees that lined the little avenues in the residential colony, a different kind of tree for each avenue. We have gulmohar on ours. Each morning in May, when I step out of the house and raise my eyes to the blazing scarlet canopy over my head, I think of the Sethji.

But it was the hospital which was his joy, his pride, his favourite child. I am sure there were many sceptics who wondered at the location of the hospital, so far away from Bombay, and in the middle, it would have seemed, of nowhere. But he was wise, the man, for here he had space, a huge amount of space. At first, the only patients were the few who came from the surrounding villages. Soon, as Bombay grew, the hospital no longer seemed so distant and referrals came from the city as well, because of the kind of doctors who worked in the hospital. For the Sethji had cast his net wide, all over the world, in fact, and snared the best he could. A list of the departments read like a comprehensive schedule of the various specialities. Nothing was spared in equipping them or staffing them. Yes, he thought of everything, our Sethji. And yet, he had left one thing out of his calculations, that one great incalculable: human feelings and emotions. For these were not just surgeons or physicians or whatever; they were also men and women. Men and women who wore white coats and an air of professional detachment and superiority. And yet, this professional armour had chinks in it. And Guru found them, the chinks, I mean. That was how it all began. Or, did it? If not, where do I begin?

'Begin at the beginning,' the king said gravely, 'and go on till you come to the end. Then stop.'

How simple it sounds! But, like everything in *Alice in Wonderland*, it's only deceptively simple. How do you know where or what the beginning is? Even our lives, do they begin with our births, or is there some earlier beginning we know nothing of? No, let me not get into that maze. Let me try to make an arbitrary beginning to my story, even if I can never trace its real beginning. Was it the day I heard Guru was coming? Yes, I could as well begin there as anywhere else. Why not?

Two

I've always thought it a strangely significant thing, the fact that happiness is so rarely used in the present tense. Happiness always *was* or *will be*. It never *is*. Now, looking back to the time before it all began, I think we were very happy then; in fact, I see our lives as idyllic. There we were, in our neat, well-built, bright, comfortable houses, with enough money, scarcely any troublesome dependants and just one or two children. We were, most of us, intelligent, liberal and modern in our outlook. Our children were healthy, they had their shots at the right time and we tried to bring them up the right way. Most of us, too, were doing the kind of work we wanted to do. What more could one want? But, looking back, I have to wonder whether there was one moment when I said to myself—I am happy.

Yes, I can remember one. And that, strangely and ironically enough, was just before I heard of Guru's coming. I had been sitting in the little sit-out outside the dining room, looking at the burnished copper of the sky from which the sun had just set. And, for no reason at all, the thought had come to me—I am happy. There was nothing more than that moment, no past, and no future. Just that one exquisitely happy moment.

And then Meera came in. I guessed it was her from the way the bell rang. As impatient as my little Sonu, she pressed her finger on the bell and kept it there until the door opened. I heard her asking Kamala, 'Where is she? Here? Manju? Oh, there you are.'

And then she plunged, as she always did, right into the thing that was on her mind, saying to me with the face of a harassed child, 'Oh, Manju, what shall I do?'

We're almost of the same age, Meera and I. Yet she always made me feel years older. Part of it was the way she looked, tiny, with the rounded softness of a child, rather than that of an adult; and her eyes, too, so open and unguarded. But more than that, it was her manner, spontaneous and direct. No evasions.

'What is the matter?' I asked her placidly, refusing to be shaken out of my mood of contentment, knowing it wouldn't be anything serious. With Meera, anything that isn't glorious is a catastrophe. There are no in-betweens.

'I'm going to have a guest,' she said, her large eyes inviting me to share the shock of this news.

Now I began to laugh. 'Since when did that worry you?'

Meera, I've always told her, is a feminist's despair. She positively enjoys being a wife, mother, cook, housekeeper and all that it involves.

'Oh, but listen,' she said, flopping into a chair opposite me, 'this isn't just any guest. It's Ashok's cousin.'

'An in-law!' I exclaimed, understanding her perturbation.

'It's not that, Manju,' Meera exclaimed irritably. 'Do let me talk. This man, he's called Guru and I've met him only once, oh, years ago. He's a rather peculiar man; he's not married, he stays in their village home and he lives like a sadhu or a sanyasi. No, no, I don't mean he's a real sadhu or a sanyasi; he only lives that way, doing without comforts. Anyway, he's got cancer and he's coming here for treatment,' Meera finished her garbled account triumphantly.

'Well, where else should he go?' I asked idly. Ashok, Meera's husband, calls it an 'occupational hazard'—people coming for treatment to our hospital and staying with us until they were better. Or dead. 'You'll have to put up with it, I suppose.'

'But Manju, listen, Ashok tells me there's no hope for him at all. He's going to die. I mean, they're going to operate on him, but Ashok says it won't make much difference, he'll die in any case.'

'Oh, I'm sorry,' I muttered.

'It's not even that,' Meera impatiently waved my sympathy away. 'What's worrying me is—how do I talk to him? What do you say to a man who's dying? What do you talk about?'

Though I pooh-poohed Meera's fears and laughed at her for having them, I found a trace of the same awkwardness in myself when Prem and I visited Ashok and Meera for the first time after Guru came to them. Prem had met him earlier, but I would be meeting him for the first time.

'Ashok's cousin is here,' Prem had said to me casually. 'From what Ashok says they were suspecting carcinoma of the stomach. Unfortunately, the biopsy has proved them right.'

'Oh, poor man! Are they going to operate?'

'Yes. And pretty soon, I guess. But how long he will live even after that is anyone's guess.'

I'd met Meera a few days after Guru's arrival at the one store on our campus, a place which sold everything. And what wasn't there, they would order for you from Bombay. It was a favourite rendezvous spot for people who were not working, something I hadn't known until I had to take leave and stay home. 'How's it going?' I had asked Meera. 'How is he?'

'Guru? He's all right. I mean, not too bad, considering what's wrong with him. But he's. . .' She tried to convey something to me, failed and tamely ended up by saying, 'It's impossible to think of him as a patient.'

Strangely, Neeta Puri, the radiologist, said almost the same thing when I met her returning from Meera's house.

'Visiting your patient?' I asked casually.

'Patient?' she wrinkled her brows.

I was never very comfortable with Neeta. Somehow she was too chic, too smart, too well-assured for that. There was something rather daunting about her. But now she smiled, showing her beautiful, slightly lipstick-stained teeth and said, 'You mean Guru? Goodness, I never think of him as a patient.'

And yet, Meera told me, she visited him every day. So did the Dean. I wondered what it was the man had. I saw it within a few minutes of my meeting him, that special quality in Guru which made the doctors step down from the pedestals they usually occupy in their relationships with patients. We found him in the living room, reclining in a large easy chair, looking like anyone else, certainly not like a man under the sentence of death. He looked a little gaunt; but then, I guessed, he must have always been thin. In fact, apart from a few pain lines on his face, there was nothing to mark him out as distinctive.

Before Prem could introduce me, he said to me, 'You're Manju.'

'Why, yes,' I replied, a little startled by the abruptness with which he said it. And then it was up to me, but I could not speak. I understood now what it was Meera had said: 'What do you say to a man who's dying?' I made a business of settling myself, saying a few words to Meera's little girls, Sandhya and Sheela, who were squabbling over something. And then, while

I was hoping that either Prem would say something, or that Meera and Ashok would join us, Guru leaned forward and said, 'Look, Manju, let's do one thing, shall we?'

'What?'

'Let's accept the fact that I'm dying and go on from there.'

I laughed in sudden relief. 'You understand how others feel, do you?'

'Yes,' he frowned, 'and it worries me that it keeps people away from me. They seem struck dumb in my presence, except for these little people,' he smiled at the two little girls. 'It puts a barrier between me and others. And now, more than ever, I don't want any barriers.'

'But there are bound to be barriers,' Prem said, speaking for the first time. 'Whether you like it or not, you are different from others. And people are always going to be wary of someone different.'

'Different? Why am I different? Because I know I'm going to die? But so are all of us. *If I die today, you die tomorrow.* Not my words, by the way.'

That, I thought, was a wonderfully brave gesture, a man speaking so easily of his own death in order to make others comfortable. I said as much to Prem when we went back home. 'It was brave of him, wasn't it?'

There was the usual pause that occurs when one asks Prem a question. 'It's his professional caution,' Ashok used to mock him. 'A pathologist is scared to commit himself. Maybe this, maybe not, or maybe something else after all—there's a pathologist's opinion for you.'

I, too, often found Prem's habit of giving every question, even the most innocuous one, its due weight and answering with deliberation, an irritating one.

'I don't think so,' he said at last. 'I think it's rather poor manners, like passing the buck to us.'

I began to laugh. 'What's the matter?' Prem asked, genuinely puzzled.

'Nothing,' I stopped abruptly, 'but it's funny, isn't it, thinking of your manners when you're dying? Rather a Kulkarni kind of thought, isn't it?'

'Possibly,' Prem said indifferently, without a smile.

Perhaps he thought it was sacrilege on my part to criticize a colleague of his, specially one as senior and important as Dr Kulkarni. But Prem hadn't always been so dour. Not with me, anyway.

'Anyway,' I insisted, with a childish stubbornness, 'I still say it was brave.'

'Well, unusual,' Prem conceded, as if giving in to a child.

Yes, that was the word for Guru. Unusual. In fact, I thought him unique. He was horribly frank and open about things, rather an enfant terrible in company. You never knew what he would say next. Pretences, even polite social ones, had no place in his life.

'It's an amazing experience,' he told me once, with a big smile. 'I can say anything and get away with it. No one dares to argue with a dying man, you know.'

There was something of the mischievous boy in him at that moment, and I could suddenly see him as one. But there was something else, too, a quality you rarely saw in people: he had the gift of breaking all barriers, ignoring all formalities and approaching you directly, as a human being. Like the way he had started off with me, as if we were old friends. I think this was what made all of us succumb to him finally. But now, sometimes, I wonder. What kind of a man was he, really? A saint, ready to give himself, his time, his love, to anyone who needed it? A brave man who had risen above all human weaknesses and crossed that dreadful barrier—the universal human fear of death? An interfering meddler who messed up our lives? I get a clue, a hint of one at least, when I remember something Guru once said: 'I know how much time I have left. Approximately, that is. And I can plan and do something with the little that's left to me. I can't leave anything to the vague future. If I want to do something, I must do it now.'

It seems to me that Guru had begun to see himself as a spectator, above and different from all of us. That's when a man becomes dangerous. Yes, dangerous, because he imagines himself God and loses his touch with humanity. And whatever Guru's motives may have been, the results were catastrophic. Two people dead, and the rest of us shattered, trying to put the shreds of our old selves, of our old lives, together again.

Old selves? No, perhaps that's not true. Not fair. Perhaps, Guru was not a catalyst who changed us; maybe he just showed us up for what we really were. And yet the thought remains—if only he had left us alone. If only he had not interfered.

Three

Guru came to us just before summer. Summer was a bad time for us. Hemmed in as we were by hills, we escaped the sea breezes. But the sea, scarcely thirty kilometres away, made its presence felt in other ways. An angry murmur at night during the monsoon. Tarnished brassware and rusted iron. And the sultriness that settled on you like a damp rug, especially in summer. The least movement, the least exertion, was enough to release rivers of sweat. But there were compensations. Cold showers, lying under the fan in a darkened room, the fragrance of jasmines, the aroma of ripening mangoes, drinking huge glasses of cold water. And for me, this year, talking to Guru.

How did Guru become a confidant? I don't know. But from the beginning, it was as if I had always known him; I could say things to him I could not to anyone else. There was the time when I said something to him that I hadn't admitted to anyone, not to Prem, not even to myself until then—my feelings about the child I was carrying.

'One child more or less,' I grumbled petulantly, 'what does it matter? After all we are—what's that phrase? Yes, *cosmic accidents.*'

Guru laughed, wincing slightly as he always did at certain movements. 'You're quoting now, aren't you?'

'Yes,' I said and, like he had done once, added, 'though I don't know who said it.'

To my surprise he immediately said, 'Jacques Monod, a scientist. Don't look so impressed. I haven't read him. I just came across those words somewhere.'

I'd heard from Ashok that Guru had not had much formal education. Yet his knowledge was astounding. But I admitted to him that I'd only heard the phrase somewhere and liked it, that I thought it very apt.

'Whatever it is, it's not right, is it, to think that way when you're expecting your second *cosmic accident* soon? But seriously, Manju, can you believe that birth, that life on the whole, is a meaningless accident?'

'What else? One sperm, one ovum coming together—it's just a matter of chance; what meaning can there be in it? Human life on this planet itself seems a bizarre chance.'

'But look, you spoke of the sperm and the ovum. Think of all that marvellous timing, that beautiful precision, the miracle of one sperm—and one sperm only—entering the ovum and the ovum then banging the door on all others. Can you call the result an accident? No, Manju, there's always a meaning, a coherence. Only if you look for it, of course. The pity is, one realizes this too late. . .'

A day or two later Guru was admitted to the hospital for surgery. He stood it fairly well. But he had a bad time during the radiation that followed. Pain-filled days and nights. Times of extreme weakness and lassitude. Bouts of high fever. Retching and vomiting. I went to see him on one of his worst days. He seemed delirious, unconscious of his surroundings. Ashok was sitting by him. He smiled at me and motioned me silently to a chair. We were surrounded by the peculiar silence that hovers over a sick room. Outside were the sounds of the usual hospital routine, but even those were somehow muted and softened; these were, after all, the special wards, not the general wards where there was constant movement, constant sound. We could hear the 'pad pad' of nurses' shoes, the swish as a trolley went by, the soft whine of swinging doors.

And suddenly Guru's eyes left the ceiling and focused on me.

'Manju,' he said loudly and clearly, 'you shouldn't—not here. . .' And his voice trailed away.

It had frightened me, I thought the end wasn't far. But Prem and Ashok seemed sanguine. 'Not bad,' they said. 'The tumour is confined to the stomach. Lymph nodes aren't involved.'

'Doctors!' Guru had said once, 'Until you die, they keep saying, You're all right, you'll be fine.'

Nevertheless, they were right this time. Guru recuperated surprisingly quickly. Soon, you wouldn't have known him for the same man; he radiated a feeling of well-being. In the evenings, he would sit on the small porch outside the house, and one by one, people would drop in. A little later, he began to walk and started visiting people himself. He usually came to me in the mornings. By then, I had started on my maternity leave and so I was at home. He would sit with me, read the newspaper, have a cup of tea.

'Peaceful here,' he said one day.

It was. Sonu had gone to her playschool, Kamala was out shopping, and Prem was at the hospital.

'Very.' I smiled wryly. 'And yet. . .' I shrugged. 'You know, Guru, every morning when I had to rush to get to the college on time, I used to think—if only I can stay home one day! Now here I am staying at home and honestly, it is getting on my nerves. I hate it.'

'That's because you didn't plan this. You don't like things going out of your control, do you? Both Prem and you like to feel you're in control.'

I looked at Guru sharply. His shrewdness always amazed me; somehow one didn't expect it from him. But he was right. What irked me about being at home was that things weren't going according to plan. Until now, Prem and I had planned our lives well. Both of us had the kind of jobs we wanted: he in the hospital as a pathologist and I as a lecturer in a Bombay college. Sonu had been born three years after our marriage, but there had always been Kamala to look after Sonu and the home while I went to work. Now Sonu was three and we had planned for a second child. But suddenly things had ceased to go right. Apart from the physical symptoms, I had a feeling of—no, not discontent, it's too mild a word. This was something worse, far worse. A pregnancy not going right could account for the lassitude, the feeling of bearing a burden, of being heavy and graceless. But it couldn't explain the sense of foreboding, the premonitions that filled me at times. As though something unpleasant waited for me round the corner.

'Oh, come on, Manju, don't be morbid,' Gautam had chided me, when I had spoken to him about it.

Gautam Kotwal was our chief gynaecologist. It may seem strange that I preferred to go to him, a male, rather than to Vidya Agarwal, our Dean's sister and as good as Gautam professionally. For me, the attraction lay not in Gautam's air of casual charm, which I secretly thought was carefully cultivated, but in his bantering. It was his levity that I enjoyed. Vidya took her profession and her patients with a dreadful seriousness.

'I've yet to meet an expectant mother who doesn't believe she's going to die. You disappoint me, Manju. I'd have expected you to deviate from the usual pattern. I guess Prem isn't cosseting you enough. That's often the case with a second pregnancy. I'll talk to him.'

He had ruffled his mop of untidy, slightly greying hair and had given me a big grin.

'Oh, it isn't dying I'm afraid of. It's just. . .'

'Just what?'

'A feeling of doom.'

'Like the Lady of Shallot, eh? See, I haven't yet forgotten my Tennyson. Now, young woman, to business.'

Gautam dropped his jocular manner and when he had finished his examination, he confirmed my fears. Things weren't going well. He wanted me to take things easy. To rest as much as possible. And to start on my maternity leave right away.

'So soon?' I had asked in dismay.

'Your due date isn't that far off, Manju. Your baby will soon be with you. A healthy baby and a healthy mother, that's what we want, don't we? Cheer up, your job won't run away. Or your students either. For all you know, they may be better off without you for a while.' Seeing my face, he had gone on more gently, 'A child born out of pain and trouble is so much more precious, isn't it?'

'Don't get sentimental and mushy,' I'd said crossly. 'I can't bear it. Just stick to your job of talking nonsense, doing nothing and then taking all the credit for a healthy baby.'

'And don't be waspish,' he'd said, unruffled by my words. 'It doesn't suit your air of dignified composure.'

'And don't try to charm me out of my peevishness, either, Dr Kotwal. Just give me my prescriptions and let me go.'

'But you're going to apply for leave right away.'

'Yes, Dr Kotwal, I will. I wouldn't dare to disobey you.'

If I had had any ideas of being the devoted wife, mother and housekeeper by staying at home, I was soon disillusioned. I realized in chagrin that I was almost a redundancy at home. Sonu had her own activities and friends and Prem had always been a self-reliant man. There was very little for me to do, either. Kamala had it all in hand, and didn't want any interference. But somehow, out of my idleness, a pattern evolved, a routine emerged. I read, I pottered in the garden, I talked to people. These conversations, if I had known it then, gave me so many clues. Clues that would explain all that happened to us and all that was soon to happen. But I did not recognize their significance then. Not until much later. It was like having different pieces of a jigsaw puzzle in my hands. Small pieces. The green of a tree. The blue of the sky. The yellow of a dress. It was only later that I was able to put them together and see the picture that emerged. What I did realize at the time was that I scarcely knew my neighbours. It was as if I had worn blinkers until then, blinkers that now came off with a shocking, startling abruptness.

There was the day I found Anand, the Puris' son, standing at the gate, looking wistfully at Sonu playing with Meera's girls in our garden.

'Hello, Anand,' I called out, 'why don't you come in?'

To my surprise, he did. Anand, at nine, looked older than his years. He had Shyam's sturdy physique and Neeta's sharp features. A good-looking boy. I offered him some biscuits and a cold drink.

'Thanks,' he said. 'Say, these cookies are good.'

'I'm glad you like them. But we call them biscuits, you know.'

'I guess you do,' he said equably, as if condoning a weakness. 'Back home, we call them cookies.'

'Back home' was the States. Well, I thought, after all, Anand had spent eight of his nine years there.

'Why aren't you playing?'

'Who's there to play with? All girls here, except Kishore and he won't play. Say, my mom tells me you're going to have a baby pretty soon. Boy or girl?'

I smiled. 'I don't know yet.'

'I sure hope it's a boy. I need someone to play with.'

'What's wrong with girls?'

'They're okay, I guess.' He gave a huge, condescending shrug. 'But they're not much fun. Look at Mriga.' In his American accent, the name was almost unrecognizable.

'What's wrong with her?'

'Aw, she's nuts. I caught her bawling this morning. Guess why?'

He looked at me expectantly. I waited a moment to give him the impression I was thinking hard. Then I said, 'Sorry, I give up.'

'Because that guy Guru—you know that sick guy, who stays with Sheela and her folks. . .?'

'Yes, I know him.'

Somehow it seemed to me that Anand didn't much approve of Guru. I was curious now.

'Well, she says he called her poor child. Mriga, I mean.'

'So?'

'That's what I said to her. So? I thought it was a crazy thing to cry about. How dare he call me poor child, she said. And she went on saying, I wish he was dead. I wish I was dead, they'll all be sorry then. Boy, she sure is crazy.'

Mriga, fifteen years old, the urbane Dr Kulkarni's only daughter, wishes she was dead?

'I guess that guy Guru's crazy himself. Know what he said to me? He said, Why don't you tell your dad you'd like to stay here? Why do you call the States home? This is your home now. Say, what business is it of his?'

'I don't think he meant to criticize you, Anand.'

'I know,' he said resentfully, a frown on his face, moodily kicking at the legs of the table. 'It's my mom, she's been talking to him about me and he tells her we should have granny, my nani, you know, come and stay with us. Dad says, no way, and Mom cries, and then they fight.'

Neeta and Shyam Puri. A radiologist and a surgeon. A perfect husband and wife team. A made-for-each-other couple. Hastily I changed the subject and led Anand away from these dangerous trails. Out of the mouths of babes and sucklings, I thought, when he went away. But more was to come to me from such a source.

It was on a day when I had just got Sonu ready, after the usual struggle with her over her milk, her breakfast, her bath, her dressing up. Often I felt like someone pushing a huge boulder uphill. And Kamala, standing by with a bland 'she-never-does-that-with-me' look, was no help at all. Now I sagged against the gate and watched Sonu trot towards Meera's house in her rompers with a cherubic face that made the last hour seem a nightmare. And there was Meera herself coming towards me. With Sheela and Sandhya running ecstatically towards Sonu, whom they looked upon as a kind of interesting, animated doll. Just then, the Shahs' front door opened and Vimala came out in her crisp cotton sari, her large bag slung over her shoulder. The picture of competence. Her house was the most spotless, her children the quietest, her garden the neatest. And yet none of us felt at home in their house. Not that we had much of a chance to be there; Vimala rarely invited anyone. She taught for a few hours each day in a school for retarded children—sorry, I should say children with 'learning difficulties', Vimala would certainly retort sharply to my calling them 'retarded'—and kept to herself the rest of the time. Now she gave us both a smile as she passed. A smile that made us feel at once idle and frivolous. At least, that was how I felt. Meera, on the other hand, was unaffected.

'Nice sari,' she said. And then, 'But an awfully dull colour, isn't it?'

I laughed. Meera herself was a butterfly, always bright and cheerful.

'Coffee?' she asked me when we went in, as if I was the guest and she the hostess. Meera was one of those persons who behave as naturally in other people's homes as they do in their own.

'Not for me.'

'I want some. Now, you just sit there and put your feet up. I'll get some in a minute. Anything for you?'

'Coffee.'

She stared at me, said, 'Oh you!' then laughed. 'Oh, all right. It's the privilege of a pregnant woman to have whims.'

I heard her chatting to Kamala in the kitchen. She had just returned with two cups when the girls rushed in shouting, 'Mummy, Auntie, Sonu fell down, Sonu's hurt.' And there was Sonu herself, her mouth a small outraged 'O', tears running down her face.

'Hush!' Meera said firmly, 'don't yell, girls. Sheela, get the Dettol from Kamala, and some cotton.'

'Sonu,' I said, 'stop crying. It's nothing, just a scratch.'

She howled all the more at that. Suddenly I was intensely irritated by her. I didn't want her to cry over such small things. Angrily I dabbed the Dettol on her knee and held the cotton swab firmly pressed there. And then, at the sight of the puckered-up face—she was taking in great, shuddering breaths now—compunction smote me. The Dettol began smarting and she gave tiny screams.

'Shall I bring a Band-Aid now, Auntie?' Sandhya asked.

'No, it isn't necessary.'

'Urmi fell down yesterday, and Vimala Auntie put Band-Aids on her. Two Band-Aids. Like this.' She held up her small fingers in a cross.

'Yes, Manju Auntie, put a Band-Aid for Sonu like Vimala Auntie,' Sheela urged me.

Sonu had stopped crying and was listening to the girls with the greatest interest. 'I want Band-Aid,' she said now suddenly.

'Tchah!' Meera exclaimed irritably. 'Don't you girls put ideas into her head. It's just a small hurt and it's clean now. No need for anything more.'

'But Vimala Auntie. . .'

'What does Vimala Auntie know?'

'She knows,' Sheela said with great dignity. 'She's a nurse.'

'A nurse?' I smiled, 'No, she's a teacher, she's not a nurse.'

'Not now,' Sheela said impatiently. 'I know she's a teacher now. At one time she was a nurse.'

'Who told you that?'

'Someone. I don't know. Come, Sandhya, Sonu, let's go.'

The girls were bored now and eager to go back to their games. I wiped Sonu's face, patted her on the back and said, 'Off you go.'

They ran off and there was a blessed silence. I was on the point of saying something to Meera, when she made a face at her coffee. 'Cold! Oh, well, it's my fate to drink my coffee cold, I suppose. Well, lukewarm anyway.'

She had just picked her cup up when I said firmly, 'Meera, put that cup down.'

'What?' She looked at me in surprise.

'I said, put that cup down. Kamala. . .'

Kamala came in. Meera was still gaping at me in astonishment.

'Kamala, pick up that cup, no, both of them, and pour the coffee down the sink. Down the sink, mind you and then make two fresh cups and get them for us.'

'Well!' Meera exclaimed, coming out of her stupefaction at last. 'What happened to you?'

'It was your using the word fate I think. No, there's no fate, Meera. There's only us. And we can control our own lives. See, you can drink hot coffee if you want to. I've proved it, haven't I?'

I still wonder, even today, why I said those words. Did I have some premonition of what was to happen? Of how our lives would be changed by things beyond our control? It's easy to surmise now. For, maybe, the truth is that it was no more than a casual statement which ended up as a joke, Meera and I both laughing at my earnestness. Drinking our fresh coffee with a rare enjoyment.

Four

The dinner at the Dean's remains etched in my memory. It was then that my vague uneasiness got a shape, a name. Prabhakar Tambe. Guru dropped the name among us, rather like a scientist demonstrating cause and effect, saying, Look, I drop a stone in this water and you will see ripples follow.

Ripples? God, yes, they followed all right.

I call it the dinner at the Dean's, but actually, it was Rani's party. It was Rani who loved entertaining and acting the hostess. She threw a party each time she came to stay with her husband. It sounds rather odd, I know, to say that she came to stay with her husband; but the fact is, it was common knowledge that the Dean and his wife had long agreed to go their separate ways. When the wife is like Rani, a woman who's made to glitter in society and the husband is Dr Agarwal, an academic and a social recluse, I suppose this is inevitable. And, being what they were, there was no ill feeling, either. Rani spent most of her time in Bombay, where she had a flat of her own, and a few months with her husband, who seemed to accept the arrangement equably. When the children, two of them, both in hostels, came home on holidays, the family stayed together. The rest of the time, Vidya managed the home, the Dean had his hospital and everyone seemed happy. Rani, too, for we often saw her photographs in glossy society magazines, smiling, a glass in her hand, and a companion, usually a male, leaning towards her.

It was Rani who rang up to invite us for dinner. Prem picked up the phone. 'Hello?' he said. Then his voice changed and he said, 'Namaste, Raniji'. So it was Rani! 'Manju?' I made faces at him. 'Sorry,' he said, 'she's upstairs. Shall I get her? Okay then. I'll do that. Yes, of course.'

I watched him smiling as he put the phone down, as if she could see him. Rani had that kind of an effect on men, even on Prem.

'What is it?' I asked him.

'She wants us to go over for dinner. Tomorrow.'

'What's the occasion?'

He shrugged and I knew he wouldn't even be curious.

'I didn't know she was back. I thought she was still in Bombay.'

'Well, she's here now, anyway.'

'Well, what did you say? Are we going?'

He had already lost interest in the subject and was leafing cursorily through a journal. Without looking up from it, he mumbled, 'What choice do we have?'

Strange how Prem made me feel invisible. No, not that, as if I didn't exist at all.

'I'd like to go. Really, I mean it.' I said fiercely and now he *did* look up at me in faint surprise.

I kept up my air of excited enthusiasm until we stood outside the Dean's house. And then, as Prem rang the bell, it suddenly deserted me, leaving me desolate and dull. The same people, the same food, the same conversation. How damnably dull life was! Or, more accurately, how damnably dull *we* made it.

Rani opened the door herself. 'Come in, Manju,' she smiled at me, 'and Prem. How nice!'

As if we were a pleasant surprise, instead of being too-often-invited and too-often-seen guests. I entered feeling huge, gauche and crude. Rani often had that effect on me. A dainty, shapely woman, with an oval face and large almond-shaped eyes, she was beautiful. And very conscious of it, indeed. She was dressed and made-up as none of us were, but it didn't make her look garish. On the contrary, it made the rest of us look pale and colourless. Her jingling glass bangles, the silver key chain at her waist, the filmy blue chiffon sari which showed her brief choli, her still-slim waist and rounded arms—all these enhanced the picture she was determined to present to the world.

'And how are you, Manju? Who's looking after you? Vidya? No? Oh, Gautam. Is he looking after you properly? I must tell him to give you special attention.'

Rani hadn't had much of an education. Her millionaire father hadn't thought his daughter needed anything but his money and her looks to make a success of her life. But nothing could make her forget she was the wife of the Dean, and I, the wife of his subordinate. But we were used to Rani, and her patronizing, condescending airs aroused nothing but a faint amusement in me. Luckily, she didn't have much time for any woman, she turned towards Prem. I went in by myself to be greeted by the Dean.

'There you are, Manju. So glad you could come.'

'What's the occasion?' I asked idly, knowing it could be nothing but Rani's boredom.

'Oh, didn't Rani tell you?' He picked a glass off the tray held out by Nathu, their efficient, almost Jeeves-like help, and gave it to me. 'Pineapple, okay? I can see Gautam watching us with that eagle eye of his, wondering what I'm giving you. The occasion? Yes, it's for Guru, you know. He's much better now and I thought we could have a small get-together. Well, make yourself comfortable.'

And he moved away, a dapper figure in the cotton bush shirt he always wore, even for the most formal occasion. For Guru, I thought. I never knew he had become that important to the Dean.

Then there was Vidya beside me, casually dressed like her brother, but elegant. If Rani was over-dressed, Vidya was painfully plain, but it suited her. 'Hi, Manju. Haven't seen you for a long time. How are things? And how are. . .?'

'For God's sake,' my voice was suddenly harsh, 'don't talk about my pregnancy and the baby. It seems to me there's nothing else anyone can say to me. Makes me feel like a breeding animal.'

'What's wrong with that?' Vidya asked me calmly. 'That's one function of life. Get it over with and you can go back to being Manju.'

How little you know, I thought. By then I won't know where or who the real Manju is. I'll only know I'm 'a mother'. But it was no use saying these things to Vidya, who'd chosen to remain unmarried.

'And relax,' she went on, 'I wasn't going to talk about the baby, anyway. With my boss looking after you, I don't need to ask. I was talking about Prem. How is he? Got over his blues? Is he going to stay on here after all? Not leaving us?'

I stared at her in surprise, 'Blues? Prem? Leaving?'

It was her turn to look surprised. 'You mean he didn't tell you? I must say I. . . I'm sorry, Manju, I raised the topic. Forget it.'

'Oh, no, you don't!' I clutched her arm and she winced. 'Sorry,' I muttered in my turn, 'but you've got to tell.'

'Well I heard from someone, I forget who it was now, that Prem was thinking of leaving us. Seemed to be down in the dumps for some reason. I was sorry. He's sound, not showy. We'd miss him and you, too, of course. Maybe I was wrong. Oh, hello Neeta. . .'

'Vidya, I wanted to see you. I tried to get you in the morning.'

'Is it about the salpingography? I've yet to see the picture.'

'You know, the patient you sent me. . .'

'By the way, Prem, have you seen those slides as yet?'

'And the prices, I tell you. . .'

'Shyam? He's always a surgeon. You should see him shaving!'

'Why these referring doctors can't write clear and simple English I just don't understand. . .'

The words, the conversation, the laughter, flowed and eddied around me while I stood there in a turmoil. Prem leaving? And why had he never told me? A marriage. You start off expecting so many things. And bit by bit, like dead leaves, the expectations fall off. But this—two people who have shut themselves off in two separate glass jars, who can see each other, but can't communicate—is this a marriage?

'Manju, hey Manju. . .' I felt a pinch on my upper arm and turned around. It was Meera. 'What's wrong with you? Standing there all alone with that sleepwalking look on your face. Cynthia's been yelling for you.'

'Hi!' Cynthia waved to me across the room.

I'll talk to Prem when I go home, I thought, as I walked across the room to her. 'Come and sit here by me.' She patted a chair next to hers with a hand as large as her smile. Nothing small about Cynthia, except her patients. A paediatrician who loved kids, with a husband who was a kind of Pied Piper to them. And they had no kids of their own; that's how it is. As I sat down, Tony came up with a small stool.

'Here Manju, put your feet up.'

'I'm all right. Don't fuss.'

'No fuss, darling. Just being sensible.'

'Really, Tony!' I said in exasperation, but smiling at him.

'These little things,' Cynthia casually remarked, 'Tony's so good at them.' There was a slight acidity in her tone that grated on my ears, but what really caught my attention was Tony's look. He was staring at Cynthia with what I can only call a hungry look. Cynthia is extremely good-looking in a statuesque way. But, for goodness sake, I thought, she's his wife. He can take her home and go to bed with her; why does he look at her like that? Then he turned away and I sighed in relief, while Cynthia went on with her usual composure, 'Did you know this was for Guru? This party, I mean?'

'I just heard that. I'd imagined it was just one of Rani's usual warding-off-boredom-in-this-wretched-little-place kind of thing.'

'He's a strange person, isn't he? Guru, I mean? My Tony has taken strongly to him. They talk for hours, though God knows what they have in common, Guru and my football-playing Tony.'

Tony was the PT and games master in a Bombay school and an excellent football coach, I'd heard.

'Humanity, maybe,' I said.

Cynthia giggled. 'Don't tell me you're getting philosophical too? Everyone seems to be bitten by that bug since Guru came.'

'Where *is* Guru? I must meet him.'

There was a babble of sound now in the room that spoke of

a party in full swing. Rani sat on the sofa, looking, as she somehow managed to do, both languid and vivacious. The Dean darted round like an energetic bumblebee, trying to talk to everyone, make everyone comfortable. Guru, I noticed, when I found him, looked excited and flushed, like a child at a party.

'So, you're the guest of honour,' I quipped.

He gave me a friendly wink, 'Nice of him, isn't it? Like a last treat.'

The words gave me an unpleasant twinge, but Guru went on in the same tone, 'But you look worried, Manju.'

'Do I?'

'Yes, you do. I can see it in your eyes. What's the matter? Whatever it is, forget it and enjoy yourself. That's what you should do when you're among friends.'

Friends? I looked around. Yes, all friends. And yet, why did I feel that there was a faint emphasis on the word when Guru spoke? As if he had put it in inverted commas?

'Come and sit here with me. Give me company while the rest of them go and eat. Ashok can get you a plate.'

'Ashok!' I snorted. 'I wonder if he's ever served himself. Meera waits hand and foot on him.'

'Oh, well, surgeons are supposed to be egoists, aren't they?'

'It has nothing to do with his being a surgeon. It's the Indian male. Look at the Shahs. Dr Shah is not a surgeon, he's an anaesthetist, but the pattern's the same, isn't it? It never even occurs to them that they might do something for their wives. They think that they've played their role by bringing home a pay packet.'

'And impregnating their wives.'

'Why, Guru, I never expected *you* to say such a thing!'

'Why? Am I not a man?'

'Of course you are, but. . .'

Luckily for me, Rani was shooing all her guests into the dining room with dainty claps of her little hands and only Guru and I were left outside. But soon people started drifting back, with their plates in their hands and Guru and I became the centre of a group.

How did we get on to the subject of crime? I don't really remember, but I know we were speaking about a trial that had just concluded. The accused, a man who had, on his own confession, killed more than forty people, had been declared of 'unsound mind' and therefore, not to be punished by the law.

'The verdict seems all wrong to me,' Guru said. 'What do you think, Manju?'

'I don't know. The primitive in me says—hang him, kill him, make him suffer. But perhaps that's not humane.'

'Humane?' Guru almost glared at me. 'How can we talk of being humane to a man who showed no signs of humanity himself? Remember how he boasted of his crimes? Was there any sign of repentance or sorrow in him? What kind of a man is that? How can you talk of being humane to him?'

'If you ask me, it isn't rational to talk of punishment in such cases.' Shyam pulled up a chair and joined us, neatly balancing his plate on his knees. 'I mean, look at it this way A man is born with something lacking in him. Call it moral sense, a capacity to distinguish between right and wrong, anything you like. Perhaps it's a chromosomal aberration which makes him that way. So, he's not responsible for what he is, is he? How can you punish him for that? Does it make sense?'

'Honestly, Shyam, you make me mad when you talk that

way! Almost like a psychiatrist. Forget your theories, forget everything. Think only of this—the man is a danger to society. He knew what he was doing, wasn't he? He admitted to the killings, he almost gloated over them, he remembered almost all of them. Which means he's responsible for his actions, doesn't it? We're always responsible for what we do. Or we should be. Otherwise, how are we different from animals?' This was Neeta.

'Trust the female of the species to be more bloodthirsty than the male,' Gautam drawled. 'So you'd like him to be hanged by the neck until he's dead, do you?'

'Of course,' Neeta said emphatically. 'Of what use is he to society? Why spend money on keeping him alive? And if what Shyam says is true, that he can never be cured, that all the psychiatrists in the world can't make him normal, what we call normal, I mean, then why keep him alive?'

'No, that's not right, Neeta. I agree with Shyam. If we think we are more civilized, if we pride ourselves on having become more humane. . .'

'Who says we have?'

'Oh, come on now, Gautam. . .'

It became a general discussion, each one eager to contribute an idea, a thought. In the midst of it, I asked Guru, 'What about you, Guru? What do you think?'

For some reason, when Guru spoke, there was a sudden silence, so that his words were heard by everyone.

'Frankly, human life seems very precious to me. Maybe I'm biased because my own life is going to be cut short. And I think of it this way: is one life more precious than forty others? I can only think of all the lives that man destroyed. Has any man the right to destroy life and not pay for it?' He paused, as if waiting for someone to speak. When no one did, he went on himself. 'What really hurts is that the man escapes the death he really deserved, while better men, of so much more use to society, die untimely deaths.'

'Better men? Who are these better men? We're all the same, all of us flawed in one way or another,' Cynthia said.

'But there are some who. . .what's the name of that man you were talking to me about the other day, Ashok? He died in your hospital, didn't he? I think you said he was a labour leader.'

Ashok hesitated for a moment, then said, 'Prabhakar Tambe. He was Shyam's patient.'

There was a slight pause, obvious only to those of us who knew how quick on the uptake Shyam usually was, before he replied, 'Yes, my patient. But first Kulkarni's, then mine.'

'And finally Prem's,' Gautam grinned.

'For the final diagnosis, eh?' Tony said, with a bigger grin.

Prem shrugged. 'Will we pathologists never live down that phrase?'

'Nearly five hundred people at the funeral, I heard,' Guru said ruminatively. 'And he died an untimely death, while this man who killed so many may escape punishment.'

'There are different kinds of punishment, you know,' Prem said, and his voice was so harsh that I looked at him in surprise. 'It doesn't always have to be—hanged by the neck until you are dead.'

'You're right about that, Prem.' Guru's eyes were—what? Watchful? 'There are different ways of paying. But no one can ever escape punishment. You pay in one way or the other.'

There was a small silence broken by a tinkling sound. Shyam's plate had slid off his lap.

'Oh my gosh, Shyam!' Neeta exclaimed in wifely indignation.

Shyam, not replying, silently got down on his knees. In a moment the Dean was with us. I hadn't seen him until then. Had he been silently listening all this while?

'Don't worry about it, Shyam. Nathu will clear up.'

But Shyam, with an unusually grim expression on his face, still unspeaking, deftly collected the pieces of china.

We broke up early, the next day being a working day. As I waited for Dr Kulkarni to finish his thank-you and good-night to Rani, I fidgeted; he was a stickler for formality and it seemed he would never finish. At last he was done; at least, I thought he was. So did Shanta, who had been standing there, stolid, silent, letting her husband do the needful. She moved away and I put on my special company smile and approached Rani. But Dr Kulkarni still stood there, staring at Rani. My God, what a look that was! I felt as if I had blundered into a room in which a couple was making love. It was a blatantly sexual look. Was I the only one to have noticed it? Had Shanta. . .? No, she had her back to her husband. It shook me, however. More so when I noticed Rani's face. She looked like the cat that got the cream. It drove all thoughts of what I had wanted to say to Prem out of my mind. I remembered it, however, when we were going to bed.

'Prem, what's this about your leaving?'

Prem was putting his clothes away and for a second his hand remained still, his trousers in his hands. 'Leaving? Who told you?'

'Vidya.'

'Oh!' He carefully hung the trousers on a hanger and, making sure the creases were right, put it in the cupboard. 'It's quite possible I said something in a low moment. You know how we talk sometimes. It doesn't mean anything.'

I did not probe any further. As I've said, ours was that kind of a marriage. But I wondered—if I hadn't told him about Rajiv, would we have had a better chance? I remembered what Prem had said to me once, 'You make a fetish of the truth, don't you? You won't tell a lie even to save someone from being hurt, will you?'

'Would you?' I had asked in return.

'Of course,' he had said, without any hesitation.

And that, I had thought later, was the cruellest thing he could have said to me; letting me in for a kind of long drawn-out torture. For, the thought was always in me after that—is this a lie? Or this? Or this? Better, I always thought myself, to have things in the open; which was why I had blurted out the truth about Rajiv and me one day. I had told Prem everything, not sparing even myself, for it was Rajiv, after all, who had backed out.

'I can't, Manju,' he had said. 'I can't go against my parents. I can't hurt them. I would never be happy if I did that.'

I had thought then that it was the end of everything for me. But not much later I met Prem and realized that life means moving on, it means putting the past behind you. I had to forget Rajiv, I had to accept that my life was now linked to Prem's.

Prem was soon asleep. But I couldn't sleep. Odd bits of the evening's conversation kept recurring. And then, suddenly, I remembered that Prem *had* spoken to me once about leaving. How was it that I had forgotten about it? And why had the memory come back to me now?

It was a night about a year ago. The bell had rung and Prem had gone down and opened the door. It had been a while before he had come back.

'Who was it?' I had mumbled sleepily.

'The Dean.'

'At this time? What is it?'

'Nothing. Just some clarification about an autopsy I had done.'

But later, when I was drifting back into sleep, he had whispered, 'Manju? Sleeping?'

'Hmm?'

'Would you mind if we went away from here?'

'Went away? Where?'

'I don't know. Nowhere, I guess. Go back to sleep.'

I had forgotten all about this incident until now. But now I remembered it—and something else as well. The autopsy Prem had done then had been of the man Guru had been talking about, Prabhakar Tambe. Yes, I remembered that distinctly. Prem had come home very late that night, with a harassed, tired face.

'An autopsy,' he had said briefly in answer to my question about why he was so late.

'Kamala says there's a very large crowd waiting outside the hospital. Who was it who died?'

'A mill worker. A kind of labour leader,' he had said, seemingly eager to be done with the subject.

He's tired, I had thought, and dropped the subject. But now it flashed upon me that Guru had brought the man's name deliberately into the conversation. And Guru had had a watchful look in his eyes. Whom had he been watching? And why?

Five

I felt like an old lady, or a retired pensioner, ambling along the road each morning. But Gautam had prescribed a little sedate exercise for me daily and dutifully I walked, each morning and evening. It wasn't very pleasant, because, even so early in the morning, it was as humid as a bathroom after a hot bath; but at least it was better than the rest of the day. The birds, however, were making the most of it; I heard the ceaseless 'coo coo coo' of the koel. I stood still and listened. Each year I heard it and yet I had never seen the bird. Perhaps that was why the magic still held. The piercing liquid tones went on and on, filling me with delight. And then, abruptly, as abruptly as it had begun, the melody ceased. I began walking again.

The door of the Kulkarnis' house opened. Dr Kulkarni, impeccably dressed in white shorts and a T-shirt stepped out, banging the door behind him. All set to play tennis. He saw me and smiled. 'Good morning,' he said. A man more English than the English, we joked. He was almost like a caricature of an Englishman, with his polite formalities, his clipped, curt speech, his perfectly idiomatic English, and his pipe. You didn't just drop in on Dr Kulkarni. You rang him up and asked if it was convenient and he did the same by you. You called him Dr Kulkarni, never by his first name, nor did he call you by yours.

'Oh, hello,' I replied awkwardly, flushing in embarrassment as I remembered his look at Rani yesterday. Had I, perhaps, imagined the look?

'And how are you? Keeping fit, I hope.'

'I'm fine.'

'Taking your exercise, I see. That's good. I'm sure you'll have a healthy boy as your reward.'

'Why not a girl?'

'Eh?' He seemed nonplussed.

'I said, why not a girl? You seem pretty sure it'll be a boy.'

'You have a daughter, don't you? I thought you'd like a boy this time.'

Mriga opened the door and ran out to where we stood.

'Maybe I'd like another daughter.'

'Well, if I were you—what is it, Mriga?'

Mriga silently held out a towel, holding it by one corner. 'Thank you, Mriga, I'd forgotten it. But what a way to bring it, child! Couldn't you even fold it? Do you have to be so clumsy? And look at your hair! What have you been doing since you got up? Mooning about as usual, I suppose. Go in and tidy yourself.'

I felt a stab of sympathy for the girl as he looked her up and down, distaste clearly showing on his face. Then he turned back to me with his usual polite expression.

'Well, I must be going,' he said courteously. 'Forgive me for losing my temper, but this child. . .'

I would have walked away too, but I hesitated, held back by the look on the girl's face as she stared after her father. There was something in it that frightened me. 'What is it, Mriga?' I asked gently.

She turned to me in surprise, as if she hadn't noticed me so far. 'Nothing,' she said, and her face closed up again.

'Having holidays, aren't you?' I asked. 'And what are you doing with yourself?'

I said it just to make conversation, but she replied seriously, 'Nothing. Just getting in everyone's way.'

It was said matter-of-factly, neither bitterness nor sarcasm in her tone. But the next moment she spoke fiercely, 'I hate holidays! School is bad enough, but holidays are worse. There's absolutely nothing I can do, there's no one to even talk to.'

And then the phone started to ring. I suppose they had it in the hall, because we could hear it very clearly. I expected Mriga to go in and pick it up. Instead, she shied like a startled animal at the sound.

'Go on, Mriga,' I told her. 'It's your phone.'

She seemed caught in a vice of agonized indecision, her eyes darting about as if she was looking for a way out of a trap.

'I can't,' she whispered, staring at me, 'I'll make a mess of it, I'll say something wrong.'

Suddenly it stopped ringing. She went on staring at me, and then taking in the silence, sighed in relief. Loudly, audibly. The tension left her face. When she spoke, she ignored the episode altogether. 'Did you mean it?' she asked instead.

'What?' I was puzzled.

'What you said about having another daughter.'

'Oh that! Of course, I meant it.'

'Oh!' She seemed to be thinking it over when her mother called out, 'Mriga!'

Shanta came out in an old faded sari, her face greasy with last night's cream, her hair dishevelled. 'Didn't you hear the phone ringing? What are you doing there? Oh. . .' she saw me, gave me a vague sketch of a smile and then went back to Mriga. 'Where's your father?'

'My father,' Mriga said, grossly exaggerating Shanta's way of saying those words, surrounding them with a halo of reverence and awe. 'He's gone. . .' and she imitated her father's accent so well that I couldn't help but smile, 'to play tennis, my dear child.'

Mriga was now as rudely, impudently mocking as a child of four or five, but either her mother didn't notice, or she decided to ignore it.

'Come in and have your bath,' she said and went away.

I wondered what it was to be Shanta, dull, colourless, a shadow of her husband. With a husband who looked at another woman in *that* way. And it was Shanta's money, or her father's money, that had given Dr Kulkarni his start, we had heard. I thought of the umpteen Hindi movies in which the heroine sang, 'I will be your shadow.' For some reason it had always angered me. How could anyone *sing* about being another's shadow, for God's sake? As if it was something to celebrate!

'Can I come and see Sonu later?' Mriga asked, an eager child all at once.

'Of course.'

I thought of the oh-so-foreign Dr Kulkarni. Behind the pipe-smoking, perfectly mannered, phlegmatic style that he cultivated, was he, after all, just a traditional Hindu male, longing for a son and heir? And taking it out on poor Mriga because she was a girl? For a brief moment, I saw Sonu and me objectively and dispassionately. And I thought, no, I'll never work out my frustrations on her. But hadn't I, perhaps, already begun? I shook off the thought and walked on. The newspaper boy was pedalling away energetically ahead of me, flinging the paper into each home from the gate, so that it fell with a loud thump. Neeta opened her door and picked up the paper on her doorstep. She straightened up, saw me and smiled. She looked warm, bright and tousled, different, somehow, from the smart, professional woman we usually saw.

'Why don't you come in, Manju, and join me for a cup of tea? Shyam isn't up yet. He had an emergency last night. It was nearly two when he came home.'

She yawned hugely. I hesitated, then went in. Anand was sitting at the dining table, concentrating on a jigsaw puzzle. He looked up, said 'Hi,' and went back to his puzzle.

'Anand's up early'

'Yes, he and I, we're the early birds. Anand, go and see if Nani is up.'

'Nani?'

'My mother's here. She came just yesterday.'

'Oh, I didn't know.'

Neeta fished out the tea and sugar canisters and yawned again. 'I'm hoping she'll settle down with us.' Why did she look defiant as she said that? 'My only brother is in Canada, you know. She stays all alone. Ridiculous, I call it. I've been trying to persuade her to come and live with us permanently. But you know how her generation is; they have a thing about living with a daughter. And she's not keeping well, either. She's a diabetic. Well, I'm going to insist this time. Anand. . .'

'What?'

'Go and see if Nani is up.'

'Mom, can't you let me finish this bit? And I wish, Mom, you'd tell her to stop calling me beta and messing up my hair. She even tried to kiss me last night.' He scowled fiercely at the memory. 'What a crazy thing to do!'

To my surprise, Neeta flared up. 'That's not the way to talk about your grandmother. Ask her to come and have her tea. But only if she's awake, mind you. Don't wake her up.'

When he went out, with an impatient, backward wave of his hand, Neeta gave an awkward laugh, trying to gloss over her anger. 'I'm worried about Anand,' she said frowning. 'He's always at home, he refuses to go out to play. Not that there's anyone he can play with. There's only the Shahs' Kishore, but you know how odd those kids are. They keep to themselves entirely. Like their parents. Oh well, I can't blame them. I suppose they haven't got over the scandal.'

I looked at her in surprise. 'Scandal? What scandal?'

'Oh, didn't you know? I thought everyone around here did. Guru seems to know about it. We heard the story when we were in the States. But if you know nothing, I suppose it's fair that I keep my mouth shut. No point spreading tales.'

Scandal? The Shahs? Vimala, utterly domesticated, wrapped up in her home, her kids and her work; and he, quiet, unassuming, coming home from the hospital and staying put after that, reading, it was rumoured, his professional journals. I was flabbergasted. And annoyed by Neeta's calm assumption that I wasn't curious. But I could scarcely pump her for information after what she'd said, so I let it alone, while she went on about Anand.

'The fact is the child hasn't adjusted to this place at all. He wasn't too keen on coming back. I can't blame him for that, really. His life in the States was the only life he knew. He had his friends, his school. And Shyam's attitude hasn't helped. He's as bad as Anand sometimes. For every problem we face, his answer is, Let's go back. Sometimes I get tired of resisting. I wish I could say, Okay, let's go. But I can't! We belong here, don't we?' She looked at me and suddenly smiled. 'Thank God for Guru. He gives me the strength to go on. If it wasn't for him, I'd never have stood up to Shyam about my mother. . .'

Dr Kulkarni and Rani. Mriga. Neeta and Shyam. The Shahs and a scandal. It was like looking through a kaleidoscope—everything was fluid, changing.

'One thing about Guru,' I said to Meera a few days later, 'he's all of a piece. I mean, there's no false façade to him.'

Meera looked up from her work—she was doing some embroidery on a dress, the complete woman, that's Meera—and suddenly giggled. 'That's what you think,' she said. 'If you only knew. . .'

'Knew what?'

'I don't know if I should tell you. Ashok may not like it.'

'Come on, Meera, tell,' I coaxed her.

'Well. . .' She put away her work. 'He was quite a character, I believe. The fun-loving type, you know. Anything but work and studies. And, as he grew older, an eye for pretty girls as well.' The smile left her face, 'I suppose it runs in the family.'

I was startled. Ashok's flirtations were well-known, but for some reason, maybe her silence, I had imagined Meera knew nothing about them. Seeing the surprise on my face, which I tried to hide, though just a bit too late, she said, 'Oh yes, I know about Ashok. I've known it for a long while. But I also know it's never serious. If I ever thought it was, I'd—I'd put a knife into him. Or myself.' She laughed, but there was no humour in that laugh. There was an awkward silence between us.

'About Guru,' I prompted her.

'Yes, Guru. Well, I believe he kept failing in his exams. It wasn't that he was stupid. It was as if he just didn't want to make the effort. And then he got a girl into trouble. Which means, I suppose, he slept with a girl and got her pregnant. The family will never spell that out distinctly. It's still very hush-hush. Why does a pregnancy become so indecent when there hasn't been a marriage ceremony, Manju? The process which leads to it is the same, isn't it? I mean, look at the way we flaunted our pregnancies! At least I did! I was tremendously proud, as if I'd achieved something. Anyway. . .' She sighed and picked up the dress again, though she didn't go on with her sewing. 'Guru, after doing what he shouldn't have, refused to marry the girl. He said, and this was quoted to me, Neither of us will be happy. They say that his father, Ashok's uncle, thrashed him. He took it silently and then disappeared. They couldn't trace him and he didn't turn up, either, in spite of the *come back, all forgiven, mother serious* notices being put in all the papers. Ten years ago he reappeared, just as suddenly and quietly. Sober, serious, ready to turn his hand to any work. He never said a word about where he'd been all those years or what he'd done. And then, this happened, I mean he fell ill. . .'

~

I couldn't help smiling at the thought of Guru's past when I saw him next. Guru had changed recently. His pallor was frightening and the smallest effort seemed to exhaust him terribly. It was as if he had drained all his reserves and there was nothing left now. Nevertheless, he was, the doctors agreed, better.

'What's that smile for?' Guru asked me.

'I was wondering how many secrets a face can hide.'

'Multitudes, I expect. We all wear masks, don't we? Though we shouldn't; I've only just realized that. To waste this one life you have in pretences, in fake emotions, is a crime. If only I had known it earlier. . .' His voice trailed off into a plaintive murmur. For the first time I heard regret in his voice. 'At one time I was dead scared of revealing myself to another person. That's what kept me off marriage, perhaps. The intimacy of a marriage scared me; now I think it's a wonderful relationship, one in which you can dispense with masks. That's what a good marriage means, doesn't it?'

'Are you asking me a question?'

'Well, yes, I am. You should know.'

I thought of my own marriage and the silences and barriers that existed between Prem and me. 'I don't know,' I said bluntly. And suddenly, shamefully, I burst into tears. I couldn't control myself. I heard the scrape of a chair and could feel Guru's comforting hand on my back. It made no difference. I shook and sobbed as if I would never stop. Finally, Guru held me close and comforted me as if I was a child. At last, I felt myself calming down; and at that moment, Prem entered. I scrubbed at my wet face and Guru went back leisurely to his chair, saying, 'Hello, Prem.'

'Hello,' Prem replied tonelessly.

And then there was a silence that seemed to go on and on. Finally Guru got up, and saying, 'I won't keep you from your lunch,' he went out. I had noticed that he rarely said any words of farewell, no, he never did.

Even after he left us, the silence continued, lengthening and stretching. Let him speak, I thought. Finally it was he who did. 'Lunch ready?' he asked. And that was that.

It was after this that things started really going wrong. For me, the weather was the worst of it. The summer seemed to go on forever. Coolness, the rains, a bed that wasn't hot and damp—all these seemed a distant dream. I felt huge, irritable, itchy and longed for my pregnancy to be over. The time of waiting seemed endless.

'Count your blessings,' Gautam quipped once, when I grumbled.

'Such as?'

'Well, aren't you glad you're not a female elephant? Imagine waiting—how much is it? Two years? Imagine waiting that long instead of just nine months.'

Gautam alternately provoked and soothed me and was, on the whole, good for me. Actually, I was much better physically. The baby was more lively now and I couldn't help responding to every little kick with a rise in spirits. The joy of living—yes, I could feel it within me and I knew that this came to me from the baby. It was strange that I could see the difference between my feelings and the baby's; we were already two different people. And, yet, so connected that, though my baby was absorbing everything from me, I felt as if I was getting a sense of eager anticipation of life from the baby.

Surprisingly I found that Guru didn't like Gautam very much. I had been praising his professional skill one day when Guru said, 'I always feel it isn't enough for a man to be skilful. I mean, he's got to be a good human being, too. Otherwise, he's incomplete, if you know what I mean.'

'Are you suggesting that there's something wrong with Gautam?' I asked, a little annoyed. 'If so, you better tell me straight off what it is. I thought you liked frankness.' I spoke a little sourly.

Guru smiled his singularly sweet smile. 'I can be frank about myself. But when the secrets are not mine. . .' He would say no more and I wondered. I wondered even more when Gautam, coming to us one day, saw that Guru was with us and walked away without a word. It was rather dreadful and I didn't know what do or say. Guru said, 'Forget about it, Manju. Don't trouble yourself about it.'

Gautam himself said nothing. He was not a man who spoke ill of others. In fact, he rarely spoke of others. His was a kind of 'you leave me alone and I'll leave you alone' policy. How little we knew about him, really! He lived alone, read a lot, had a weakness for Hindi movies—that was about all we knew. But what had Guru done to Gautam that Gautam should walk away from him? For the first time, I realized that everyone didn't see Guru as I did. That he wasn't the same person to others as he was to me.

I'd heard of a pregnancy bringing a husband and wife together. With Prem and me, it seemed to have the opposite effect. We had drifted even further apart. Unlike my earlier pregnancy, this time I felt as if I was alone in my struggle to bring my child to life. I don't know whether Prem had sensed this feeling of mine, but he kept himself aloof. He looked after me with the detached kindness of a stranger. We had even, I realized one day, stopped quarrelling, as if we did not even have any areas of disagreement between us.

And then one day, something flared up between us. Sonu was the innocent cause of it all. Since my pregnancy, the child had moved away from me. After being constantly warned not to bother me, she had stopped coming to me with accounts of her daily activities, her little anxieties. In a way, it was a relief, but there was a sting in it too, specially when she went so easily to Kamala, brushing me aside, even when I offered to help her. It humiliated me to see how much better she was with Kamala than she was with me. Meal times, specially, had become a torture. Nothing worked, neither threats, nor persuasion, nor bribes. She clenched her teeth, set her soft baby lips in a determined line and shook her head to everything. Her resistance infuriated me and I felt I had to break it down.

My desperate attempts to control my temper usually gave way and ended in tears on my part and tantrums on hers.

'Leave her alone,' Prem said. 'Stop fussing over her and she'll eat.'

'She won't, she'll starve.'

'Let her.'

'How long?'

'Don't be silly. No child will ever starve.'

I'm a failure, I often thought. I can't manage my own child. Perhaps this baby would be different? But I couldn't fool myself; there would be no difference, I would go on making the same mistakes. We can rarely help being what we are. And that, I thought, is the real meaning of fate: inevitability, which comes from being what we are.

That particular day Sonu had been much better behaved. Mriga, who had developed an affection for Sonu, had taken her out. On coming home, she had eaten her dinner without any fuss and I had been very pleased with her. She got ready for bed and I reminded her to go to the toilet before going to bed. She hesitated. 'Go on,' I said encouragingly.

'No,' she said frowning, 'I want Kamala.'

'Kamala's busy,' I said, stifling a small spark of irritation. 'You're a big girl now. You can go by yourself.'

'I want Papa.'

'Papa's busy.' My good humour was giving way. 'Go on.'

'No.'

The child refused to budge. The struggle between us became fierce and ridiculous; for some reason I couldn't let her off. She began to sniffle, saying, 'Papa, Papa.' Her tears and moans irritated me, I didn't want her to grow up a clinging vine. I wanted her to be fearless and independent. When I tried to make her climb the stairs, prising her small fingers from the banisters, she began to scream, shrill high-pitched screams that drove me mad. I pushed her, knowing only that I had to make her obey me.

And then Prem came to us. 'What is it? What's going on? Sonu, what's the matter? Why are you screaming like that?'

Hearing her father's voice, Sonu flew to him and clutched him round his legs, sobbing and hiccupping, while I stood where I was, all anger drained out of me. I was filled with remorse when I saw how the small body trembled, how the child clung to her father for protection against me.

'What is it?' Prem turned to me for the first time.

'Nothing,' I said wearily. 'I wanted her to go to the toilet alone and these tantrums are the result.'

'I. . . I. . .' Sonu's voice quavered and shook like her body as she tried to speak.

'For God's sake, leave her alone,' Prem shouted, glaring at me as if he hated me. I had never seen him so furious. Without masks—is this how you want it to be, Guru? No, better to have them on. Far, far better.

'Can't you see she's scared?' he asked, one hand holding Sonu's sobbing little body close.

'Scared? I don't want her to be scared. I don't want her to become a whiner. I want. . .'

'*You* want this and *you* want that! Can't you ever see anyone but yourself? Not even your own child? What kind of a woman are you, for God's sake, to do this to her? Leave her alone. Let her be what she wants, let her do what she wants.'

'Yes I'll leave her alone. Leave her to you to spoil and pamper.'

Prem ignored me completely. He bent down to Sonu and

picked her up. As he carried her away, murmuring soothing words, it hurt me to see her hands clasped tightly round his neck. I stood there alone and desolate for some time. I could feel my heart pounding loudly. I couldn't just stand there. I had to do something.

I got out of the house, closing the door softly behind me. It was a dark night. There was a hint of a breeze, a whiff of freshness outside, which hadn't penetrated into the house. But there was no comfort in anything. I walked on blindly, blankly, my mind a deep well of misery. I don't know how long I walked, or how far I went. I came out of the fog only when I heard a voice say, 'Why, Manju?' Even then, I could see nothing but Sonu, clinging to her father, looking at me with fear. And Prem glaring at me. For all of us there comes a time when we can no longer hide our knowledge of what we are from ourselves. Now I was looking at myself and I hated what I was seeing.

'Out so late? And by yourself?'

Dark clouds were scurrying across the inky black sky. A pale moon peeped through for a second, showing me the Dean. Dully, I responded to this recognition, showing neither interest nor embarrassment, though I could taste salt on my lips and knew I had been crying. And I knew, from the way the Dean spoke, that he had seen my tears. As I tried to take in his words, to reply to him, I began to come back to normal. And then I realized the Dean looked odd as well, he didn't look his usual self. I couldn't pinpoint the difference, but the feeling was there.

'Are you going back home?' he asked me gently.

Was I? Yes, where else could I go? But was I going home because there was no other place? And yet, what could I do?

There was Sonu. And the child to come. For a moment, I resented them bitterly. Motherhood, I thought—it's a trap. Keeping you in a cage until you lose the desire for freedom, until you forget what the word 'freedom' means.

'Yes I'm going back home.'

'Come on, I'll give you company.'

We walked on in silence for a while. I roused myself to ask him, 'Are you going to the hospital?'

'No, I'm going to see Ashok. Ashok rang me up. It seems Guru wants to see me.'

'Is anything wrong?'

'No, he's all right. As all right as he can ever be, I mean. It must be something he wanted to speak to me about. Well, here we are. Don't go wandering that way in the dark again. You'll have Prem worrying. Goodnight.'

'Goodnight.'

Prem worrying! I could have laughed. But he opened the door the instant I rang the bell, as if he had been waiting for me.

'Where were you?' he asked me angrily. For some reason, his anger pleased me. 'Sonu wants you. She's been crying for you.'

Oh, that was it! I should have known.

Sonu's voice came to me from her room. 'Have you come, Mummy? Have you come?'

'Yes, my pet. I'm here.'

I sat by her and kissed her soft, warm, wet cheek. 'Why are you crying?'

'I thought—I thought you went away. I thought you won't ever come back.'

'Silly child! I'm not going anywhere. I won't go anywhere without you. I'm here. Go to sleep.'

She held my hand in both of hers and gave a soft sigh. Soon her hands relaxed their hold on mine. I sat beside her for a long time, crouching awkwardly. At last, I covered her and went into our room.

Prem was lying in bed reading. He didn't raise his eyes from his book when I entered. I brushed my teeth, washed my face, changed, folded and put away my clothes. Then I drank some water and got into bed. Prem was still reading, seemingly unaware of my presence. My heart felt as cold and heavy as my body. The bulge of my body, which no blanket could hide, disgusted me and for a minute I hated myself and the child I was carrying. I felt it move, as if protesting against this emotion. I closed my eyes and tried to sleep. For a long time I lay with my eyes closed, but wide awake. It was not just unhappiness; there was something else, a kind of fear hovering over me, a feeling of something dreadful waiting for me round the corner. The fear was almost palpable. I could almost smell it, touch it. Prem was still reading, steadily turning the pages over, when I finally drifted off into sleep.

Six

I woke up the next morning full of determination—a determination to do something that invariably succeeds a night of misery. I would go and see Cynthia, I thought, I would talk to her about Sonu's problem and ask for her advice. The very thought made me feel more cheerful.

I rang her up. 'Why don't you come home?' she said. 'Today? Lunch time? I'll be home early. Twelve, is that okay?'

When I got there, however, she hadn't yet returned from the hospital. Tony was alone at home.

'Hi, Manju, come on in. Want to see Cynthia, eh?'

'I didn't expect to see you, Tony. Enjoying your vacation, huh?'

'Vacation? What vacation, Manju?'

'Summer vacation, isn't it?' I asked in surprise.

'No, not for me. I'm having a longer vacation that that. They've given me a summer, winter, monsoon vacation all rolled in one. Don't have to go to work for a long time.'

For the first time, I realized that Tony was a little drunk. Not drunk, really, just a little tight. But at this time of the morning? I was surprised. I had never seen him this way before.

'They booted me out. Didn't know that, hey?'

'I suppose you'll go on to another place then,' I said.

'Yeah, yeah, going to get a much better job,' he said, waving his hands expansively, vaguely. 'That was a stupid little school. No good, no, no good at all.'

'Well, I'm sure you'll get something better.'

I looked anxiously at the clock. I hoped Cynthia would come soon. I didn't look forward to meeting Prem at lunchtime, I dreaded the silent meal, but I didn't want him to think I was avoiding him, either. I felt I had to be home when he came.

'Of course, I will. What do you think I am? I almost made it on the national team, you know. Nearly made it to the Olympics once. Almost did so many things. Now. . .' He dropped abruptly from bragging into self-pity. 'Nobody wants Tony. Poor old Tony. Nobody wants him. He can be Cynthia's husband. That's enough for him.'

'Can I have some water?' I asked awkwardly. Anything to stop him.

'Sure, sure. Why just water? You can have anything you want. Say the word, just say the word, I'll get it for you.'

'Nothing more,' I said firmly, 'just water.'

When he came back with a tall glass, full to the brim, I noticed he looked flabby, as if his muscles had gone slack.

'When do you think Cynthia will be back?'

'Should be here soon. Never know, though. Busy woman, my wife, you know. Oops, sorry.'

The water had slopped over. He seemed genuinely concerned about the pool on the carpet. He was kneeling down, dabbing away at it with his hanky, when Cynthia entered.

'Tony!' she said sharply, 'What are you doing?'

Without looking up, still making small ineffectual dabs, he said, 'Can't you see? I'm kneeling, I'm proposing to Manju. My favourite girl, you know.'

'Sorry, Cynthia,' I interrupted him, seeing the look on Cynthia's face. It was mortification, not anger. 'My fault, I'm afraid. I just spilt some water.'

'Hi, Manju! Sorry to keep you waiting, dear. Leave it, Tony, leave it, I said.' Her voice rose again.

'Okay, okay,' he said amiably, staring at his wet mop of a hanky.

'Have you had your lunch?'

'No. I was waiting for you.' Tony got up, avoiding looking at her.

'Come on then, let's start. Manju, do you mind if we talk as we eat? I've got to rush back, I'm afraid. Tony, will you see that lunch is on the table?'

Tony obediently shambled out and even as I opened my mouth to speak, to say that I would come back some other time, Cynthia said sharply, 'What was Tony saying to you?' There was a tiny pucker between her brows.

I looked at her in surprise. 'Nothing, really. Oh, yes, he was telling me about his job.'

'Oh that!' She seemed relieved. 'I'm not really worried about that. He'll get another job any time he wants. He's good, you know. If only he gets himself in hand. It's just that I'm worried about. . .' It seemed as if she would go on, then she changed her mind and said, abruptly, 'Oh well, let's forget about it. Now tell me about Sonu. Don't tell me the pet isn't well?'

Theories, I thought bitterly as I walked home. It's easy to theorize about children: don't fuss over her, don't nag at her, ignore her tantrums, don't be harsh. But children have a habit of scattering our theories to the winds. Anyway, I thought, I can at least try it out.

Prem was already home when I got in. It was as if last night's quarrel had never happened. But can one ever erase anything as completely as that? There was an uneasiness between us that could not be ignored. So that when Prem came back early from work, I found myself foolishly dreading the long evening that lay ahead of us. And then the telephone rang. It was Ashok.

'He wants us to go to their place,' Prem said. As I hesitated, he added, 'Actually, it's Guru, I believe, who wants to see us. Shall I say we'll be there?'

'Of course,' I said instantly, relieved at the thought of going out; and yet, I wondered uneasily, why did Guru want to see us? I was full of a Cassandra-like foreboding as we walked to Ashok's place. To my relief, however, it was just a social occasion.

'It's for no reason at all. You can call it a sudden impulse,' Guru said, smiling at me, as if reassuring me. Had he sensed my fears? 'Meera said she was bored and we planned this between the two of us. So, here you are, all of you.' He spread out his hands, taking us all in. Yes, there were Neeta and Shyam, too, going into a huddle as usual with Ashok and Prem. Talking shop, if I knew the four of them. The Shahs had their invariable strained social look, while Gautam looked relaxed, as always. I was a bit surprised to see him, remembering the day he had turned his back on Guru. But here he was with us, though I noticed he rarely went near Guru. The Dean and Vidya came in directly from the hospital. The Dean, ignoring everyone, went straight to Guru. Rani came in later with Tony and Cynthia.

It was a surprisingly pleasant evening, except for that one incident. But that came later. At first, Meera's cheerful informality pervaded all of us. There was no elaborate meal, just a variety of snacks set out on the table, to which people helped themselves with gusto. Meera was a good cook and enjoyed seeing people eat. She beamed as the plates were emptied and refilled them with enthusiasm. Dr Kulkarni came in while we were eating. He came alone and I heard him elaborately apologizing to Meera for Shanta's absence.

Guru stayed put in his chair, but there was always a group around him. Different people at different times. The electric lights emphasized his gauntness and pallor, giving him a skeletal look. His face had a guarded expression now, the look of a man who constantly nurses pain. He didn't stay with us for very long. He went to bed early. Ashok and Meera helped him in and then Meera came out saying, 'He's gone to bed, but he says we should go on, nevertheless.'

I had had just a few minutes with him. 'How's Sonu?' he had asked, as if he knew that she was my main worry at the moment.

'Problems,' I had said.

'Tell me.'

'Not now,' I had said, looking around.

'Okay, come round. Tomorrow morning?'

I nodded.

But the next morning he was dead. I woke up to the strident sound of the phone ringing. It was Ashok. Guru was dead. He had died in his sleep.

Seven

I put the phone down and shivered in the small hall, dank with humidity and heat. But I had to wake Prem up and tell him about it. 'Tell Prem I want him,' Ashok had said, cutting off all my questions by putting the phone down. I walked back to the bedroom, feeling clumsy and bulky. I began to shake Prem.

'Wake up, Prem, wake up.'

He rolled over on to his back and stared at me, his eyes open. He seemed to be returning from some distance.

'Prem,' my lips trembled, 'Guru's dead.'

He sat up abruptly at that, awake and alert in a moment as usual. 'Guru? Dead?'

I nodded.

'When?'

'In his sleep last night. Ashok rang up. He wants you there at once.'

There was a silence. Prem had a strange look in his eyes. It was as if he was still taking the news in, trying to understand its implications. Then he spoke. 'It was expected,' he said.

I felt a flare of anger within me, but I controlled myself. 'Ashok wants you there. At once,' I repeated.

'Okay.'

He got out of bed and groped for his slippers. 'I'll just brush my teeth and go,' he mumbled.

I began to make the bed. I folded the sheets, spread the cover and smoothed it mechanically without thinking. And then all at once, I felt an onrush of grief. I won't cry, I thought, remembering the last time I had cried and Guru had comforted me. And Prem had interrupted us and said nothing. I remembered, too, how Prem had, when hurrying out just now, halted at the door and looked back at me, as if there was something he wanted to say. But he had said nothing, just turned away and gone out. I had seen something in his eyes, though, that had hurt. Was it pity for me? I won't think of these things right now, I told myself. I hastily bathed, dressed and gave some instructions to Kamala before going to Meera's place.

The house was quiet, as if its inmates were still sleeping. The subdued bustle that comes into a house after a death hadn't begun as yet. Meera burst into tears as soon as she saw me. 'Oh Manju, it was such a shock,' she said, as she was to say to everyone. 'Just imagine, he was perfectly well last night. Who would have thought that this would happen?'

I let her cry for a while, then I said, surprised by my own composure, 'A good way to go. You know how worried he was that it would go on and on. That he would become just a suffering animal kept alive by the doctors.'

'I know, but. . .' Meera had finished with her bout of tears. She wiped her eyes and face roughly, as if determined to shed no more tears.

'Sandhya and Sheela?' I asked.

'They're still sleeping. They don't know as yet.'

'Why don't you send them to Kamala? She'll look after them. I've spoken to her about it.'

'Will she? Shall I wake them up?'

'I think you should. Before people start coming in.'

But she held back. 'What shall I tell them? Why don't you tell them, Manju?' She looked like a girl asking to be let off a distasteful task.

'I couldn't, Meera. You have to do it yourself.'

Reluctantly, she went out of the room. I went into the dining room and sat erect on one of the straight-backed dining chairs. My hands were trembling. I locked them tightly together. I could hear voices coming from the bedroom which I knew was Guru's. Once I heard Prem's loud voice, as if raised in anger. For some reason it scared me. I sat there like a frightened child until Meera came back.

'They've taken it surprisingly well,' she said. 'Thank God for the blessed matter-of-factness of children. They're brushing their teeth. What about their baths?'

'Kamala will manage. I'll go up and help them to get ready. Don't you worry about anything, you'll have enough to cope with. It's going to be a long day for you.'

As I went upstairs, I could hear subdued voices in the hall. The scraping sound of footwear being removed. It was beginning.

The girls were in the bathroom. I could hear them conversing, 'shhing' each other when their voices rose to their normal pitch. Quick footsteps came up the stairs. It was Neeta. 'Where are the girls?' she asked me.

'Getting ready. I'll take them home. Kamala will look after them.'

'That's fine then. But my mother's offered to have them, too. In case Kamala can't cope. . .'

'Oh, she'll love to have them. They enjoy Sonu, you know.'

'Okay, then. Shall I walk them over to your place? Save you a walk.'

Behind this small talk, I could feel a kind of restrained anger in her that puzzled me. Why was she angry?

'Sheela?' she called out, taking my agreement for granted.

'Yes, Auntie?'

'Have you finished?'

'Coming. This silly Sandhya takes such a long time to brush her teeth. Just because your teacher told you to brush hundred times, you don't have to go on brushing for hours.'

'Ssshh, don't shout. Don't you know Guru Uncle's dead?'

They came out, their faces shining and scrubbed, but deliberately subdued. And yet they couldn't suppress their excitement entirely, a natural reaction to the change in routine, to the sense of importance that surrounded them. They left eagerly with Neeta, towels and clothes in their hands, as if they were going for a swim. I heard them clattering down the stairs. Neeta, lingering a little, said to me, 'Just twelve hours ago, we were all here. We knew he was going to die. Why, then, Manju, do you think I have this feeling of being cheated?'

Cheated? Yes, I thought, that's the word. Guru had taken us by surprise. Death, yes, but not now, not today, not like this.

I sat there for a long time in the girls' room. It was utterly peaceful. I dreaded the thought of going down, of seeing Guru, of having Prem's eyes rest on me with that look of pity in them. Someone came up now slowly. It was Vimala. I was surprised to see that her eyes were red with weeping. Why had *she* been weeping for Guru?

'Where are the girls?' she asked me.

'Neeta has taken them to my place.'

'Oh!' she said and relapsed into silence, making no move to go back down. I heard Tony's voice downstairs, raised, as if in annoyance. And suddenly, I realized why Vimala had come up here. The girls had been just an excuse; she wanted to avoid Tony and Cynthia because of what had happened between her and Tony last night.

I thought of the scene between Vimala and Tony. It had happened after Guru had left us to go to bed. We had wanted to watch a panel discussion on TV which was about hospitals and health issues. Meera had switched on the TV and put out the lights. Tony and Cynthia had come in while we were watching the programme. Rani was with them. Tony and Cynthia would have just quietly joined the rest of us, but Rani made such a business of, 'I don't want to disturb you, do go on, don't bother about me,' that we soon gave up. In any case the reception was poor. People split up into small conversing groups after that. I was with Vimala when Tony joined us.

Earlier, hearing his loud laughter, it had already crossed my mind that he was, once again, not too sober. But he looked pretty much as usual, his face flushed and damp with the heat, his multicoloured shirt clinging to him with his perspiration.

'Hi, Tony,' I smiled at him, 'How's life?'

'Wonderful, as you can see,' he said, making an expansive gesture. He had his plate in his hand and as he waved it, the fork fell down on Vimala's foot.

'Oh, sorry, sorry, sorry.' He knelt down to pick it up and began to prod at Vimala's foot, pushing her sari aside. 'Have I hurt you? Let me see, let me see.'

Vimala drew back her foot and, hiding her annoyance with a visible effort, said, 'I'm all right.'

'No, no, it's not all right.' Tony was still kneeling, still scrabbling vainly for Vimala's foot. 'Let me see what I've done. Show me I haven't hurt you, tell me you forgive me.'

Oh God, I thought in dismay, Tony was really high. High?

No, he had obviously gone way past the ceiling. But Vimala, to my surprise, had been furious. I could have warned her that it wasn't the right way of dealing with him at the moment, but she had gone on, too angry to care. 'Please don't make a fool of yourself,' she said grimly.

He got up at that. 'Okay, if that's the way you want it. But if that cut gets infected or you get te-te-te-tetanus,' he brought it out finally with a triumphant air, 'don't blame me. But of course, you can look after yourself, can't you? Once a nurse, always a nurse, isn't it, darling?'

'Don't call me darling.' Vimala, who had been holding herself in with rigid self-control, almost spat out the words. 'And I'm not a nurse. I never was one.'

Tony had given a huge sigh. 'She doesn't like me,' he said to me with a faint self-pitying air. 'She doesn't love me. But nurses are like that. They can only love doctors. Doctor-nurse romance, hey?' And then he had belched and said, politely, 'Excuse me.'

'I'm not a nurse, I never was a nurse,' Vimala repeated with a touch of hysteria in her voice.

Tony had begun to laugh at that. For a man of his size, his laughter was ridiculous. A high-pitched giggle that turned into a silly whinny. Cynthia had turned round sharply at the sound and was with us in an instant. 'Come on boy, let's go home.'

'Home? And the party just beginning? Just because this lady, this ex-sister doesn't like me? Let me tell you, Madam,' and now Tony was immensely dignified, 'I don't like you, either. I don't like liars. I'm a God-fearing, truthful, honest man. That's what my dad always told me to be. Tony, he said to me...'

Cynthia had tugged at Tony, murmuring, 'Tony, please.'

Ineffectually, because, even if he was flabby, Tony was still a powerful man. It was Ashok who had persuaded him, finally. He had come to Tony and said, 'Come and lie down for a few moments, Tony.' And Tony, surprisingly, had gone like a lamb, pausing for an instant to fling a last dart at poor, stricken Vimala. 'A liar, am I?' he had glared at her. 'Ask Guru. He told me. He knows about you.'

I had looked at Vimala when Tony had gone. The angry colour on her face had faded and she had been looking about, as if for someone. It had been her husband's eye she had finally caught in a kind of agonized plea. She looked frightened to death and on Dr Shah's usually mild face I had seen violent anger.

Now, Guru was dead and Vimala was unaccountably hovering in the Sandhya and Sheela's room, shattering the spurious peace that had surrounded me until then. I wished she would go. She gave me the feeling that she was here because there was something she wanted to say to me. Finally, when she spoke, she just repeated Neeta's words: 'Just twelve hours ago, he was here.' And then, reflectively, 'And now he is dead.'

It gave me a shock to hear a faint note of satisfaction in her voice. I couldn't bear to be with her any more. I'd rather see Guru's dead body than be here with her, I thought

We sat around and made uneasy conversation while we waited for Guru's elder brother to come from Poona. People kept coming in all the time. We had never known until then how many friends Guru had made. Rani was there, dressed dramatically in stark white. She looked like the chief mourner. Ashok, oddly enough, had locked himself into one of the rooms with Prem and the Dean.

'I wonder what's going on,' Meera whispered to me. Her

face, I noticed, was as peaceful as a child's after a bout of weeping. I envied her her child-like resilience. Vidya, tense and brittle-looking, kept an anxious gaze on the door behind which we could hear the voices of the three men. People went to the hospital for brief periods, for emergencies, perhaps, and came back.

Mriga turned up suddenly, a short while after her mother joined us. Her father saw her first. 'Mriga,' he said, 'what's the matter? Why are you here?'

With so many eyes on her, she was more confused than ever. She coloured, swallowed desperately and seemed unable to speak. Her father's crisp anger reduced her to total incoherency.

'Go home,' he said. 'You know this is no place for you. Shanta. . .'

Shanta moved obediently towards Mriga. But before she could do or say anything, Meera went to her and, taking her by the arm, led her in. Meera gave me a pleading look as she went and I followed them. As soon as we were out of the room, Mriga wrenched herself out of Meera's grasp. 'You don't have to hold me like that,' she said with an odd dignity. 'I can go home by myself. I won't run away.'

'Mriga, I'm not trying to send you home,' Meera said.

'Aren't you?' She looked suspiciously at both of us. Then she asked with a pathetic air, 'Have I done something very wrong in coming here? Why does he talk as if I've committed a crime?'

'Well, you know, Mriga, deaths, funerals—these are not pleasant sights. Certainly not for. . .' Meera hesitated, I knew she was going to say 'children', but she finally said '. . .young people.'

'I've a better right to be here than he has,' she said defiantly. 'He hated Guru. I've heard him talking. Guru was my friend. I was angry with him at one time, I said nasty things to him. I'm sorry about that. That's why I thought I'll come here and. . .'

'We all say things we don't really mean, Mriga,' Meera said. 'I'm sure he knew you didn't mean it.'

'He was. . .' her nostrils quivered, 'he tried to be kind to me. I was nasty to him.' She wiped her eyes with the back of her hand and gave a sniffle of misery.

'Mriga,' I spoke to her for the first time, 'would you like to go to our place? Sonu's there, Sandhya and Sheela have gone there as well.'

'You mean, to play with them?' she asked me.

'Goodness, no! To help Kamala with the girls, if you feel like it.'

'*She* says, Go and play—as if I'm Sonu's age.' I knew she was speaking of her mother. 'How old does she think I am?'

Shanta came in now. Mriga, without looking at her, said, 'I'd like to go to your place. Shall I?'

'Of course.'

She ran out, without a word to Shanta. Shanta went out silently.

It was after noon when they took Guru away. It's over, I thought. I would always associate Guru with this period of my life, but there would be, I hoped, no aftertaste, no lingering memories. It was finished and done with. How little did I know that this was only the beginning of the nightmare!

~

I went home, had a bath and was lying down, totally exhausted, my mind a blank, but taking in with pleasure the voices of the little girls playing downstairs, when the bell rang and the chattering voices suddenly stopped. The next minute, footsteps clattered on the stairs and the girls rushed in, Sheela saying, 'Vimala Auntie has come.'

'Tell her to come in here, Sheelu,' I said.

'Are you okay?' Vimala asked, taking a chair by the bed.

'I'm okay. Just this backache.'

I don't think she heard me. Her enquiry had been merely perfunctory. 'So he's gone,' she said and this time there was no satisfaction in her voice. The words were flatly, plainly stated.

'Yes.' The word dropped, heavy as a stone between us. I thought of Guru for one last time as a living presence. And then he became the past.

Vimala seemed oddly nervous. She said nothing for a while. Nor did I. Then, abruptly, as if she was plunging into cold water, she said, 'Manju, you heard Tony say some crazy things to me, didn't you, yesterday?'

I knew now what was coming. Confidences, revelations. Why me, I wanted to ask? Why are you telling *me* things? Once you tell me, you'll never want to talk to me ever again. I don't want to hear you, I don't want to know anything. But Vimala was all keyed up to unburden herself; I couldn't have stopped her even if I had tried.

'If I was you, I'd forget it, Vimala. You know he wasn't all right. He didn't mean it, I'm sure. . .'

I smiled, but Vimala didn't smile back. Even at the best of times there was no humour in her. 'He called me a liar,' she said flatly. 'And he was right. I did lie. I was a nurse once. I must tell you, you'll understand why I had to lie.' She looked tragic. 'I knew it would happen. Rumours, they've followed us everywhere, wherever we've gone. Yes, even here. I was afraid, always afraid. That's why I kept the children isolated. Suppose they heard something? I couldn't bear that.'

There was a long silence. She stared down at her hands. Suddenly she looked at me. 'Tell me, Manju, what kind of a man was Guru?'

'Guru?' I was bewildered by the sudden switch in the conversation.

'It's because of him—I don't want to talk ill of a dead man, but it was he who. . . You heard what Tony said, didn't you?'

'What did he do, Vimala? Guru, I mean?'

'He knew about us. I told him myself one day. He seemed so sympathetic and I was so tired of the burden.' Her eyes went back to her hands again. She was weaving and unweaving her fingers as she spoke. 'It seems such an old story to plague us still. Sumant was married then.' This was the first time I was hearing Dr Shah's first name. 'His wife was no good for him. I'm not just saying this because. . . I mean, she was really no good. She was a pampered child who never grew up. I felt sorry for him. We became friends. I was working in the same hospital, you see. There was nothing wrong with our relationship. It was perfectly innocent, I swear. And then she died. She committed suicide.'

She gulped and her eyes moved to the wall. She stared at it, as if she couldn't look me in the face. 'They had had a quarrel over some trifle. It wasn't because of me. I mean, I wasn't in the picture at all then. She always threatened suicide when she couldn't have her way. He'd got used to it. This time she really did it. It was suicide, I swear it was. But people began to talk. Specially when Sumant and I—Sumant and I. . . He was lonely, all broken up by her death. He kept blaming himself, but what could he have done? People think he's reserved and cold. He's not, he's very sensitive, really. He couldn't get over the thought of her suicide. He was in a bad state, he needed me, so we got married. Then I began to get anonymous letters saying that I—that we—had murdered her. We left that place and went abroad, our kids were born. It's fifteen years now, but the story still dogs us. We can never leave the past behind us. It follows us everywhere.'

There was a prickling of sweat on her forehead and upper lip, though we were sitting right under the fan. I felt desperately sorry for her.

'But Guru?' I asked hesitantly.

'Don't you see? He knew about it. He was the only one. Lately I felt people were looking at us strangely. You heard Tony yesterday, he said Guru had told him. Perhaps he told others too. Guru was constantly after me, saying, You can't run away forever, Vimala, you're harming your children by keeping them isolated. If you're innocent, why panic? Let the children know from you. Don't let them hear about it from others. He kept saying these things to me.' Vimala looked fierce. 'I'd never let that happen. I'd do anything to prevent that.'

'But Guru wouldn't. . .' I was beginning, when she interrupted me. 'What do you know about him? I'm telling you he wanted me to let everyone know. Once it ceases to be a secret, you're free, he said to me.'

'That does sound like him,' I agreed.

'Why did he interfere? What business was it of his? It's our secret, isn't it?'

'Vimala,' I said, 'Guru was right. Tell the children about it yourself. Don't let them hear it from others.'

'I won't, I can't,' she said passionately.

She left soon after, both of us painfully embarrassed by these revelations. It was impossible to resume a normal conversation after this.

Revelations! There was worse to come before the day ended.

Eight

The same night, we had just finished our dinner, actually it was our first meal of the day, when Ashok came in. Rather, he rushed in impetuously. 'Can I speak to you, Prem?' he said, without giving me a glance. They went out and I sat there, feeling as resentful as a child kept out of adults' secrets. Idly, I turned over the pages of a book, without taking in a word of what I was looking at. It was nearly half an hour before they came out. Ashok left after a few words to me; the usual civilities, nothing more. As if ours was a formal relationship! I felt a shiver of apprehension when I saw Prem's odd expression. I waited for him to say something. When he didn't, I asked him, 'What is it? What's the matter?'

He gave me a level, considering look before replying, 'It's about Guru. Ashok thinks there's something not right about his death.'

'Not right?' I asked, totally puzzled. 'What do you mean?'

'He says—the idea is so preposterous that I feel a fool even to put it into words—he says he doesn't believe Guru died naturally.'

I still couldn't grasp it. 'But he was ill, I mean he was suffering from cancer. He did have cancer, didn't he?'

Prem leaned forward, his face unusually gentle. 'I don't

want to upset you, Manju, but this thing is sure to get round. And I've never seen Ashok this way. He's so determined, I can't seem to get through to him at all. To me, it seems ridiculous. This morning, I'd actually thought we had got it out of his head. . .'

'Got what out of whose head?' I asked, angry because nothing seemed to make sense. I felt a hideous fool.

'An autopsy. Ashok wanted an autopsy done on Guru.'

'But why?'

I must have seemed enormously dense and slow to Prem. But he was still patient, still gentle, as he explained. 'He thinks Guru was given something which caused his death.'

Now, at last, it penetrated. 'But that would be murder!'

It was like using a strange word, a word I didn't really know because I'd never used it before. A word that belonged to books and newspapers and movies. What had it to do with us? And yet, as soon as I said it, it became ominously familiar.

'I knew it would shock you,' Prem's face came back into focus. 'I can't believe it myself. I can't imagine how Ashok got the idea into his head. When I went there this morning, he was standing and staring at Guru. It's all wrong, he kept saying, it's all wrong. The Dean, Shyam and I had a job dissuading him from asking for an autopsy. Now, he says he was wrong to have given in to us. I agree. If nothing else, it would have proved him wrong, it would have got the suspicion out of his mind.'

'But Prem', my voice came out a croak, 'there has to be some reason for him to feel that way.'

'Reason?' Prem's face was grim. 'A man needs no reason for believing what he wants to believe. Actually, Ashok can give us nothing concrete. No proof. Just a feeling. Guru, he says, was quite all right last night. There was no reason for him to die so suddenly. But Ashok seems to be ignoring the huge fact of his illness. He knows—who better?—how quickly and suddenly a cancer patient can go. Like a match in the wind.'

'There must be something else,' I insisted stubbornly.

'Yes,' Prem reluctantly admitted, 'there is. It's Tony. That's what Ashok came to tell me about. Tony went back to Ashok's after the funeral. I wasn't there at that time. It seems Tony created a scene. He said he knew that someone had killed Guru. One of us.'

There was a cold feeling in the pit of my stomach. I stared at Prem dumbly for a moment. Then I burst out, 'No! No! Who would want to kill Guru? Who could have done such a thing?'

Prem's smile was so frosty, it frightened me. 'I don't know about the second question, Manju, but I can answer your first one. Plenty. Plenty of people who would have wanted him dead, I mean. I myself,' the smile became a grimace, 'often wished him dead.'

Looking at his face, I knew he wasn't joking. And there was nothing I could say after that.

'Well,' he shrugged, 'let's hope this doesn't get around too much.'

What a vain hope that was! In a short while it was all over the campus. Rumours floated over us, light as thistledown, but suffocating us all the same: Guru has been murdered, Ashok believes it was murder, Tony says the same thing, they killed him and then they had a party, Guru was a saint, he was a blackmailer—and so on and on and on. It was difficult for us, who were involved, to talk about it. But it was even more difficult to avoid the subject. There was the day I went to Gautam for my usual check-up and he was not in.

'He'll be back soon,' the sister assured me. 'You want to wait?'

'I'll wait,' I told her. 'You can go back to doing whatever you have to do.'

But that was the last thing she wanted to do. She wanted to talk. I didn't respond, but that didn't deter her. She carried on a monologue. Starting with Gautam and how busy he was, and how the other sister never kept things in order, she adroitly steered the talk to Dr Kulkarni. 'Poor man,' she said, with a huge, very obviously false sigh, 'I wonder if he now feels sorry for what he did.'

'What was that?' I couldn't avoid the question, though I knew I had been led up to it.

'Why, I thought everyone knew about it. About the way Dr Kulkarni treated that poor man, Dr Prabhu's cousin. The one who died recently. I was there that day and heard him myself. Dr Kulkarni, I mean. My, was he angry! He was red with anger, you know and shaking all over. I won't stand for interference, I tell you, he was shouting. What right have you to talk to me that way? It's none of your business, understand that. I wondered who he was shouting at. And then I saw it was Dr Prabhu's cousin. Is it true there's something funny about his death?'

'I don't know,' I said coldly.

To my relief, I heard Gautam's quick steps. 'What's the matter?' he asked me, looking at my face when we were alone.

'Gautam, do you think it's true? About Guru, I mean. The way people are talking, honestly, it scares me.'

'Guru. . .' Gautam said, looking down at the pen he was rolling in his hand. 'I'm tired of hearing his name. How I wish he had never come here.' The pen suddenly broke into two in his hand. He stared at it unseeingly for a moment, then, tossing the pieces into the wastepaper basket, said briskly, 'Well, Manju, how are things now?'

And I knew he would say no more. Looking at him washing his hands, scrubbing them rather, I felt he was literally washing his hands of the whole affair.

The story about the Shahs had suddenly come out in the open. Everyone seemed to know about it, God knows how. Dr Shah, we could see, was trying to keep up a normal facade, but Vimala had turned into a hunted animal. She was rarely seen out of the house.

'I tried to talk to her once,' Meera told me, 'and she snapped at me like I was harassing her. I was only trying to help.'

I could believe that; Meera was totally without guile.

And there was Neeta. She had lost her poise and calm almost overnight. She had a tense and brittle look and there were dark circles, almost like bruises, under her eyes. She had turned into a chain-smoker and was rarely seen without a cigarette in her hand. There were strange rumours, hinting at a foundering of the Puris' marriage and linking this to Guru's death. But both Neeta and Shyam kept a resolute silence.

These were, however, just stories I heard, in varying degrees of distaste and disbelief, and shrugged off. I couldn't do the same when the shadow fell over us. It was nothing anyone said. Rather, it was the way they avoided speaking to us. To Prem, especially. Always a falseness in the tone, a forced heartiness. It seemed to me that everyone was looking askance at Prem. I tried to tell myself that it was only my imagination. But there was the way Meera had changed. Normally as candid as a child, she was now subdued with me, oddly silent and with an air of unnatural reserve about her. I often felt that she was on the brink of saying something, yet she never did. Ashok and Meera had been our closest friends, but they had stopped visiting us or inviting us home. This didn't hurt me as much as it frightened me. There was no one I could share my fears with, least of all Prem. What was it, I fearfully wondered, that had changed him into this silent and morose man? I couldn't ask; his face kept questions at bay. And now, there was no Sonu to act as a buffer between us. I had sent her away to my mother's, making my health an excuse. It had been a difficult decision, but I had felt that she was better away. Hesitantly, I had broached the subject to Prem. To my surprise, he had welcomed it. The child was full of joy and excitement at the thought of going to her grandparents, her uncle, aunt and cousins. It gave me a pang to see her leave so happily.

'Where's Sonu?' Anand asked me the next day, as I was pruning my rose plants. I pushed my hair off my face and looked at him. Hands clenched into fists in the pockets of his jeans, he looked a sturdy and tough boy. But there was something wistful in the eyes that looked at me over the hedge.

'Sonu? She's gone to her grandparents in Bombay.'

'Oh!'

'Did you want her?' I asked.

'Aw no!' he said casually. Then, adult-like, 'She's a nice kid.'

'I suppose so,' I smiled.

A thorn pricked me. I sucked at my finger. We stood in an awkward silence for a while. Then suddenly Anand said, more cheerfully, 'Say, you know something?'

'What?'

'You know that guy my mom thought a heap of? That guy Guru. . .?'

'Yes, Anand, what about him?'

'He died, didn't he?'

'Yes, he did.'

'But I bet you don't know how he died. He was. . .' He leaned forward and hissed the words at me, '. . .murdered.'

'Oh!' I looked at him and tried to compose my face. 'How do you know?'

'Oh, everyone does,' he said, with a faint scorn for my ignorance. Suddenly losing interest in the subject, he asked me curiously, 'Why are you cutting those plants?'

'It's called pruning. They grow better if you do this.'

'Guess they did it to Mriga,' he grinned. 'That's why she's that tall.' And then he seemed to remember something. 'Say, that girl knows something. About Guru's death, I mean. I told her he was murdered. And she said, It's all rot. Why should anyone murder him? But she knows something herself. Know what she was doing the other day?'

My questioning look was encouragement enough for him.

'She was burning something in their backyard,' he said, lowering his voice to a conspiratorial whisper, 'and she was crying. And when I asked her what she was burning, she got scared, sort of, and said, Nothing. Go away, you snoopy kid. *Me*! A snoopy kid!' He looked utterly indignant and went on darkly. 'Maybe she murdered him herself. And was burning evidence.'

'You know that's all nonsense, Anand,' I hoped I spoke in a matter-of-fact, no-nonsense voice. 'Do you know what this rose is called?' I asked, changing the subject.

'What?'

'It's called King's Ransom.'

'Why?'

'Because it's so beautiful, I guess. There! I've finished. I'm going in for a cup of tea. Like to join me?'

'Thanks,' he said politely, 'I never drink tea.'

'What would you like to have?' I asked him.

'I don't know. I wish we could get some pizzas around here. My mom makes them at home, but they're not the same as the pizzas back home.'

'No, it can't be the same.' It was Neeta; I hadn't seen her coming. For some reason, she was in a flaming fury. 'This is India, remember, not the US? It can't be the same. How many times do I have to remind you that *this* is home? And that this is where we're going to live?'

He frowned, and sticking out his lower lip mutinously, kicked moodily at a pebble. 'Not for long,' he mumbled, 'we're going back home, I mean Baltimore, soon.'

'Who says so?' Neeta asked sharply.

'Dad.'

'No, you're not.'

'I am. Dad promised me we will.'

'Come in, Neeta,' I said, hoping to end it there.

'No, thanks. Some other time. And Anand, come home right away yourself.'

It was this way now with all of us. Always, 'Some other time.' Everyone seemed wary, on guard. Yet no one admitted openly to any uneasiness. We tried to keep up a front of normality, but we knew we could not keep up the pretence forever. The bubble had to burst. And one day it did

~

We were all at the Staff Club that day. It was a Saturday, and by tradition, most of us went out that day. Sunday was the day for the club. But that Saturday, there was a magic show arranged for the kids, and most parents were there, waiting to take their children home. Prem and I were there because we had nothing to do at home. And, maybe, because we didn't want to be on our own. I went straight to the magazine rack and picking one, began to read it, though desultorily. Prem went and sat by Shyam. Meera came in a little later and sat down near me. Squeals of excitement and delight came to us from the hall as the magician performed his tricks. After Meera had asked me about Sonu and I had made my inquiries about Sandhya and Sheela, there seemed to be nothing more for us to say to each other. It was weird how far we seemed to have moved away from our earlier selves. Meera and I having nothing to say to each other! I'd have laughed at the idea earlier.

I was relieved when Ashok came in a little later. His eyes picked Meera out, and giving me a small smile, he asked her, 'Haven't they finished yet?' She shook her head mutely. He gave an exclamation of impatience and looked at his watch. 'I'll be back soon,' he said and was striding out of the room when someone called, 'Ashok, hey Ashok!'

It was Tony's voice which came from one of the large cane chairs at the other end of the room. He was slouching in it, which was why, perhaps, we had not seen him. Prem and Shyam, who had been carrying on a low-voiced conversation, looked up sharply on hearing Tony's voice.

'Come here, man.' Tony's slurred words carried their message clearly across the room. He was drunk. It was strange how fast he had begun going to pieces. Ashok stopped where he was and Tony's grizzly head appeared over the chair. He leaned heavily on it, got up and began walking towards us, an idiotic smile fixed on his face.

'Hi, Ashok,' he waved and said, 'So here you all are, eh? A

happy family. Innocent people. Not a worry on their minds. Not a sin in their hearts.' Tony was obviously being deliberately provocative.

Ashok set his chin and gripped Tony firmly by the arm. 'Now, now, Tony, not again. If you aren't feeling well, you better go home.'

Impatiently, brusquely, Tony snatched his arm away. 'What's this nonsense about going home, man? I've as much right to be here as all of you. Am I not a member of the family of one of the staff?' He articulated these last words slowly, with great care and precision. 'Just because I'm a little—a little. . .' Now he faltered, as if he had expended all his energy on his earlier words and had no more left. He finally ended with 'a little tight', bringing the words out triumphantly and grinned at all of us. '. . .you can't keep me out. Come on now, who wants to turn me out?' He was suddenly belligerent. 'Come and try it, I say. Come on, fellows.'

He was met with a dead silence. Ashok, I noticed fearfully, was raking all of us with a critical look. His eyes lingered on Prem and my heart lurched in panic. Why do you look at him like that, I wanted to cry out. But I was as silent as the rest of them. The children's excited cries, their laughter, provided an incongruous backdrop to our silence.

'No one dares to touch Tony, eh? And why?' He turned round smartly, like a soldier on parade and faced Ashok once again. 'You know why, don't you, fellow? It's because Tony knows. He knows something. He knows about you all. Bloody killers. Killing a dying man who never did anyone any harm. Complacent bastards, he shook all of you up, didn't he? Guru did that. He told me about it. You doctors—you think you have a license to kill?'

'Oh, come now, Tony,' Ashok said with an unconvincing

laugh, while the rest of us stayed mute and still. I remembered the game of 'statues' we had played as children. Staying silent, immobile. As much as a small twitch and you were 'out'. Who would get 'out' now?

Tony irritably shook off Ashok once again. 'Oh, get off it, man. Leave me alone,' he said. 'I know about you, too. You and your little sweetie from the theatre. Phoo.' Tony made a sound of disgust. 'Bringing her home—think I didn't see her that day? I saw you both together. And poor Guru lying there, dying.'

There was a rasping sound, like a piece of cloth being ripped. It was Meera. She burst into tears and while all eyes turned from Tony to Meera, she buried her face in her hands and sobbed. I stared at her aghast, then put my arm round her. But she wrenched herself from my hold and saying, 'No, no, no,' ran out of the room. Ashok, his face expressionless, followed her, ignoring all of us.

The silence that followed was broken by a grotesque sound. It was Tony giggling. He went on and on, as if he couldn't stop. Prem got up and went towards him.

'Tony,' he said.

Tony stopped laughing as abruptly as he had begun. 'The great pathologist, huh?' Prem looked steadily back at Tony. 'Your job's laying bare the truth, isn't it? What about that bloke, Prabhakar? What about him, man?'

Prem's eyes dropped. He moved away from Tony. And then Cynthia entered. 'Tony!' She took it in, Tony standing there and glaring at Prem, the rest of us obviously in a state of shock. 'What's going on?'

The next moment the doors of the hall opened and the children streamed out, an excited, chattering crowd. 'Manju Auntie,' I heard Sandhya's shrill voice, 'where's Mummy?'

Nine

It wasn't long before everyone knew about the scene at the club. As for me, for some reason, from that day on, I had no doubt at all that Guru had been killed. And by one of us. The conviction had come, not from Tony's drunken truculent speeches, but from the silence with which his words and accusations had been met. The silence had continued even later, as if there was an unspoken conspiracy between everyone to ignore the matter. But the questions buzzed ceaselessly in my mind: why had Guru been killed? And Prabhakar Tambe—what had he to do with the matter? And how was Prem connected with it? I had seen his body stiffen when Tony had said the name Prabhakar. Maybe I should have asked him the same day. 'Prem,' I should have asked, 'what's it about the man Prabhakar Tambe?' But there had been no words between us as we had walked home that night, and when I woke up in the morning, it had somehow seemed too late.

And there was something else, too, that kept me silent: the fear of being rebuffed. If Prem refused to answer my questions, it would be a dreadful confirmation of what was already becoming clear, that Prem and I had moved far apart. But even worse than this was the fear that I would hear something I would rather not know. 'I myself often wished him dead.'

How often those words of Prem's came back into my mind! It seemed to me that I could never get away from them.

And yet it was impossible for me to remain in such total ignorance. I had to know. Perhaps Ashok would tell me if I asked him about it. There was no one else to whom I could admit my inability to talk to Prem. I decided to meet Ashok away from his home, or ours. I had not met Meera since that dreadful day at the club. I found myself increasingly reluctant to meet her as the days passed. Better, I thought, to meet Ashok in the hospital.

Ashok's habits and timings were both erratic and uncertain. I knew, however, that he had his outpatient on Thursday mornings and that he stayed on in his room in the afternoons, doing the paperwork he rarely had time for on other days. He would be alone then. Ideal for my purpose.

'The doctor in?' I asked one of the peons, lounging outside Ashok's room.

'Yes, he's there,' the man said, with a peculiar smile on his face. There was something disagreeable about it, but it didn't really penetrate. I was preoccupied with my own thoughts, thinking of what I was going to say to Ashok and wondering whether I was going to get anything from him. Perhaps, it was because of this that I neither knocked, nor had myself announced. I walked straight in and found Ashok and a woman in the room. They were standing, facing each other across the table, looking in some way like two antagonists. There was a sudden silence at my entrance. The woman had been crying. The tears were still on her cheeks. I didn't know her, but her face seemed familiar. Surely I had seen that serious, intense, sensitive face somewhere? And then it came to me—I had failed to recognize her because she was wearing a salwar kameez. I had seen her in her uniform, the face framed under a nurse's cap.

Ashok, who had been glaring at her, turned to me and focused the same angry look on me. 'What the hell. . .' he began. Only then he realized who it was. He pushed his hair off his forehead and said, 'God, Manju, I didn't know. I'm sorry. . .'

The woman stood still, not bothering to wipe the tears from her face. She didn't look at me, not after the first glance. Her whole being, it seemed to me, was entirely concentrated on Ashok; she could take in nothing else. There was something painful about the intensity with which she stared at him. I had the odd discomfort one gets in the presence of another person's intense suffering. He's made a mistake, I thought; she's not the woman for a light flirtation.

She stood there as if she would stand in that spot forever. 'You can go, sister,' Ashok said trying to speak calmly, authoritatively. She didn't move. 'I said you can go.'

'I can come back some other time. . .' I began awkwardly, when Ashok angrily interrupted me, 'No, Manju, don't go.' And then, turning to her, he repeated, 'Leena, go. Why don't you go?'

At that she stirred. There was a faint smile on her face, as if she had won some victory. Perhaps it was the fact that he had called her by her name. 'All right,' she said, 'I'll go, but. . .'

'For God's sake, just go!' Ashok exclaimed in intense anger.

Her face, as she walked out, was tragic. It moved me intensely. I could scarcely bear to look at Ashok. He sat down in his chair, as if his legs had suddenly given way. 'God!' he said. And then, 'Sit down, Manju. Please.'

'Ashok. . .'

'Look, Manju,' he looked at me eagerly, appealingly. The

old irresistible Ashok. What woman could resist him? Had that been his undoing? 'It's not what you think it is.'

'Isn't it?' I asked him coldly. For the first time I thought of Meera and the way her eyes lingered on Ashok whenever she saw him. And this woman. . .

Ashok was awkward and confused. 'You've just got to believe me. I mean it. It isn't what you think it is. For God's sake, don't go and speak of this to Meera.'

That really infuriated me. 'You should know me better,' I said, not hiding my anger.

'I'm sorry,' he mumbled.

'And I must say, Ashok, it's damn cheeky of you, expecting me to believe you. I've heard about this. . .'

'But it's all over. Believe me, Manju, it is. Since Guru came. . .' There was a long pause.

'Yes?' I said encouragingly.

'I don't know who told him about it, but he spoke to me of it one day. I told him that for me it was just a bit of fun, you know. After all, what's wrong in talking to someone you work with?'

Bit of fun? I looked at Ashok in horror. How could a man be so stupid?

'I told him that for me there was only Meera. She's the only one who matters, she and our girls. And imagine, this woman wanted me to give up Meera and the girls for her! Imagine me giving up Meera! Giving up my daughters!'

'What if Meera had decided to give you up?'

'Oh, she wouldn't,' Ashok replied, looking unforgivably smug. 'She knows me, she understands me.'

The whole situation was so stereotyped it was almost a cliché. The way Ashok saw it, I mean. He was the erring, yet loving husband, Leena, the 'bad' woman, the seductress, the temptress, and Meera, the good and forgiving wife. Ashok had the three of them neatly compartmentalized. Yet there was something wrong, something he had missed out. I thought of Leena's face, of Meera's sobs the other day. . .

'Really, Ashok, I can't understand you,' I said despairingly. 'How could you?'

'Don't preach, will you?' he said irritably. 'I don't owe you any explanations, do I? God knows why I'm trying to explain. Just forget about what you saw.'

He gave me a pleading look. What could I say? And there was Meera, she was my friend.

'And what about her? Leena, I mean. Can't you see she's dead serious about you? Can't you see she's suffering?'

'Oh, she!' he said airily. 'She'll forget me fast enough. She's married, you know. She has a husband in the Middle East, she gave me the usual flap about being lonely, about her husband not understanding her. That's how I—I mean, I was just being friendly and sympathetic. She misunderstood me.'

I said nothing and he went on, 'She'll go back to him. She'll be all right,' he said confidently. 'I was just telling her to go to her husband when you came in. Actually, I haven't spoken to her for ages. I had promised Guru I wouldn't have anything to do with her. I was already tired of her emotional tantrums. A bit of cheerful conversation, a little innocent flirtation is one thing. This sob stuff gets me down. But she wouldn't take it from me that I didn't want to have anything more to do with her. She wouldn't leave me alone. She kept trying to meet me. She came home that day, you know, the day before Guru died. Imagine her guts, imagine her coming home! Suppose Meera had seen her! I could have killed her,' he said easily. 'Thank

God, Meera didn't see her. I was taking Tony to lie down when I saw her at the side door. Gave me a shock to see her there. Somehow I managed to get her out of the house. She wanted to see Guru, she said, not me. She was getting hysterical. She kept blaming Guru for my refusal to see her. I've got to meet him. I've something to say to him, she kept saying. I told her Guru was sleeping, I took her to his room, she saw him sleeping. It was only then that she agreed to go away. The next day, Guru was dead.'

So she had been in the house, too, that night and Tony had seen her. Perhaps, she had gone back into Guru's room, after Ashok left her and. . .I came out of my thoughts to find Ashok regarding me with a shamefaced look. Like a boy caught with his hand in the biscuit tin. 'You do understand, don't you?' he asked me.

'I? How do I matter? I'm not important. It's Meera you have to think of.'

'Oh, Meera,' he said again. 'She understands me.'

How dare you take her for granted, I thought angrily! But it had nothing to do with me. It was between Meera and Ashok. And anyway, I had no time for Ashok's affairs now. I remembered why I had come to Ashok. 'Ashok,' I said abruptly, 'What's it all about? What has Prabhakar Tambe to do with what's happening? And what has Prem to do with it?'

'Prabhakar Tambe?' he repeated the name thoughtfully, questioningly.

'You remember how Guru brought his name into the conversation that night at the Dean's? And Tony mentioned him, too, the other day. What is it, Ashok?'

'Why don't you ask Prem?' he said, obviously stalling for time.

'Prem? He's became a deaf mute. We talk of nothing but the stupidest trivialities. Any letters? I'm going out. Where are my glasses? Things like that. Nothing more. You've *got* to tell me, Ashok. There's no one else I can ask.'

Ashok was silent for a while, fidgeting with the things on his table. The fan was on full blast, ruffling his hair, lifting it, giving him a carefree look, which his expression totally belied. A page of a calendar on the wall flapped violently, loudly, rhythmically.

'I can't, Manju,' he said at last. 'It wouldn't be fair. You've got to ask Prem. There's nothing I can tell you. No facts, that is. All I have is surmise.'

His eyes were speculative. He knew something. But he wouldn't tell me. Nor would Prem. That left only Tony. And it was Tony who told me something after all.

Ten

It was time for the monsoon rains to begin. Day after day, dark, brooding clouds hung over us, stifling the atmosphere, but there was no rain. For me, it had become almost unbearable, the heat, as well as the humidity. I passed sleepless nights, thinking of cold streams, soft winds and grey skies. If only I could go away! But there was nowhere I could go. And something kept me stubbornly near Prem, though at times it seemed that he scarcely knew I was around. He had taken to going to work even earlier than usual and coming back late. One evening I could no longer bear being alone in the house, I had to get out of it. I wandered about in a desultory manner, not wanting to meet anyone or talk to anyone.

I saw Tony near the football ground. Some boys were kicking a football about and Tony sat there on the railings that lined the grounds, watching them. Hands in pockets, hair blowing straight back with the breeze, he somehow looked lonely and forlorn. On an impulse I walked up to him.

'Hi, Tony.'

He turned round. He looked thinner—though maybe that was an illusion—and sober. He gave me his usual friendly smile. 'Look at that fellow, Manju. He's good. The others are just okay.'

We stood in a companionable silence for a while. Tony got off the railings and said, 'Let's sit down on the grass. Take your weight off your feet. Some considerable weight now, eh, Manju?'

He helped me to lower myself and thankfully, I sat down. 'You'll have to help me up,' I said and Tony grinned. 'No problem. I can even carry you home. You and your baby.'

In a moment he went on, obviously thinking aloud, 'Sometimes I wonder if things would have gone better between Cynthia and me if we'd had a kid.'

I was silent. 'Guru tried to help us, but it didn't work. Cynthia didn't like him. She called him an interfering fool. I wonder if she was right. It's a fool's business, interfering with others. Even Guru said that one day. I'm tired, he said. Let them stew in their own juice. But he was a decent fellow. He cared about others. How many of us do? There was nothing I couldn't say to him. Even about Cyn and me.' He paused.

'I didn't know Cynthia and you had a problem, Tony,' I said. 'You seem so wonderful together.'

'Problem?' He stared straight ahead, his eyes narrowed, a frown on his face. 'So little really for two people who want to make a good life together! But without kids, we didn't seem to have the heart, somehow. We got along fine at first, Cyn and I. We had our jobs, we loved each other and that was that!'

Odd, I thought. He's speaking as if it's all over between Cynthia and him. It scared me. And then, he spoke with more animation. 'Don't let them tell you it doesn't matter who earns more money in a marriage, Manju. It does. There was Cyn before marriage, crazy about me, looking up to me, ready to do anything for me. It didn't matter at all that I was only a hockey player, a good hockey player, but still, just that. And she was a medico. We were crazy about each other. God!' he swallowed. I saw his Adam's apple move up and down. 'I don't know if you've felt it, Manju, but these doctors, they get to thinking they're above other humans. Perhaps it's having human life in their hands that makes them feel like gods. Maybe it's the patients looking so much up to them, maybe it's the habit of instructing. I don't know what it is, but they get that air of authority, of superiority, all right. I started feeling that Cyn was patronizing me.' He sighed heavily. 'Oh well, I don't know! Sometimes I think I should go away. It's no good for me, this life, I mean. I have my parents in Goa. They're old now, they'd love to have me back. I could easily get a job there too; any one of the football clubs would gladly take me on. It's like a dream calling me, my parents' home, the beaches, the churches, that old way of life.'

Twilight had crept in on us. The players on the field were calling out to one another loudly, indulging in a bit of horseplay, preliminary to winding up. I had never seen Tony this way. I hated to spoil things but I had to ask him the question.

'Tony, what do you really know about Guru's death?'

He came out of his reverie with a visible start. In the dim light, his face looked wary, watchful. 'Why do you want to know?'

'I've got to know, I've just got to. Tell me, Tony, for God's sake!'

He put his large hand on mine, pressing it painfully into the ground. 'Relax, girl, relax. It isn't good for you to get into such a state.'

'But you will tell me?' I persisted.

'Okay, I'll tell you.'

~

By the time he finished, it was dark. His face was just a blur.

'Is that all?' I asked.

'Isn't that enough?'

'But there's no proof.'

'I'm getting it. Just you wait a bit, Manju, you'll see. And Cyn, too. She'll realize that Tony isn't such a dolt as she thinks he is. She looks at me these days as if I'm an idiot child. I can almost see her classifying me, trying to gauge my IQ. But she'll soon know what I really am. I'm going to see that the bloody person who did this to Guru doesn't get away.'

I tried hard to make him tell me what was on his mind. If only he had! But who can look into the future? How could he, or even I, have imagined what was waiting for him? I left him there full of plans, gleeful as a child at the thought of showing Cynthia how clever he was. My way back home took me through the clump of mango trees that surrounded the temple, a temple built, according to the Sethji's wishes, on traditional lines, complete with sunken tank and a stone pillar for the lights. In the daytime it was a cheerful place, with the continual ringing of the bell by the worshippers who flocked to it. Now, however, it seemed dark and eerie and I regretted having come this way. Then I heard the murmur of voices. I smiled to myself, reassured. A courting couple, I thought. This was a favourite spot among the students. So many marriages must have been made here, and so many hearts broken as well. I heard a laugh now and stiffened. Rani Agarwal! What was she doing here? I felt as if I had stumbled on something dirty and began to hurry. Suddenly, I felt myself collide with someone. I gasped, my heart lurching into my mouth. I caught hold of something. An arm. There was a sound of surprise, an exclamation.

'Mriga!' I almost sobbed in relief, having recognized the voice.

'You saw them? You saw them?' Her eyes gleamed in the dark. I could sense that she was on the brink of hysteria. She clutched me tightly while she went on, 'I saw them, I followed them. They didn't see me, but I saw them. They were. . .' She hiccupped, laughed and choked in the same breath. I shook her wildly. 'Mriga! Calm yourself, Mriga. Come on, let's go home.'

'Home?' she wrenched herself free. 'Yes, I'll go home and bring my mother here. I'll show her. Let her see him now, let her see what he's doing.' She almost spat the words out. I tried to hold on to her. But she twisted away from me and fled. I was left there, listening to the stumbling footsteps crunching on the dry leaves. I felt I had to get away myself. I felt somehow as if I was surrounded by malignant shapes. I walked fast and reached home, drenched in my own sweat. Prem was sitting in the hall, he looked at me in amazement.

'What is it, Manju? What is it?'

His voice came to me from a distance. I sank into a chair, I could not speak. He took me in, helped me to change and made me go to bed. He brought me some hot milk and sat by me as I drank it. And then I knew I had to say it, though it would destroy the new gentleness in him.

'Prem, you must tell me about Prabhakar Tambe.'

'Prabhakar Tambe?' He stared at me, the empty glass in his hands. 'Who's been talking to you? Who?' He put the glass down carefully. 'Is it Tony?'

'Tony didn't, I mean, Tony didn't want to say anything,' I stammered, frightened by his face.

'Didn't what? The drunken idiot! The damn fool! He's asking for trouble. What has he been saying? What?'

His face hung over mine, magnified, distorted. He took off his glasses and his eyes looked opaque. I shook off my fear and with a fury equalling his own, turned on him. 'He told me nothing. You have to tell me. You.'

The only reply was a slam of the door. I lay in bed and turned my face into the pillow, feeling drained out, unable even to weep. Prem hadn't believed me, but it was true. Tony had told me nothing about Prem and Prabhkar Tambe. 'It's for Prem to tell you that,' he had said firmly.

In the middle of the night, the rains broke. It came down like a thunderbolt, pounding the roof and windows in a wild frenzy. Prem came in drenched. I heard him moving about as he changed.

The next thing I knew was that someone was screaming. I got up with a start. The bed beside mine was empty. And the screaming was real, it went on like a fearful siren. I stumbled downstairs, clutching my gown about me. Vidya and Prem were supporting Mriga into the house. They laid her down on the sofa. Her eyes were wide open, full of some horror. So was her mouth, though she was not screaming now.

'What is it?' I asked fearfully.

It was Mriga who replied 'Tony Uncle—he's dead. He's floating in the tank near the temple.'

And then she burst into loud, uncontrolled sobs. They were a relief after the screams.

Eleven

The situation now had the quality of a nightmare, horror and a feeling of unreality grappling with each other. The pictures were distorted, confusing, overlapping one another, resulting in a meaningless, frightening jumble. I felt as if I was seeing a horror movie being run through at great speed. There were faces and sounds and movements, all of them unrelated to one another. There was Neeta's face, gaunt and ghastly, Vidya's, grim and silent, Prem steadily cursing God-knows-whom, until he suddenly stopped and said, 'My God! Cynthia! We've got to tell her.'

But someone must have told her, for there she was with us, looking unbelievably tall in her wrapper, bending over Mriga, saying, 'Don't be scared, child. It's all right.' And then, she straightened herself out to her full height, towering over all of us, and asked Prem, 'Is it true? Is Tony. . .?'

'Yes,' Prem said very simply.

Neeta put out her hand as if to touch Cynthia. But Cynthia, with a little gesture, withdrew from us, her face unchanged, and said, 'Leave me alone. Please. I must be alone.' And then she walked away, her step as unhurried as usual, while we watched her helplessly. I moved as if I would follow her, but Prem held me back by a gesture, saying, 'No, don't, leave her alone.'

Now the room was full of people. Dr Kulkarni was one of them, apologizing, my God, yes, apologizing to us for the trouble Mriga had caused, for what he called her 'unbalanced behaviour.' I could scarcely bear to look at him and screamed, 'What kind of a man are you? Look at the child! And you apologize to us!'

Shanta gave me a curious look then. I thought that, perhaps, she was shocked. Maybe in her eyes I had committed sacrilege, speaking in that way to her husband. But Neeta putting her arm round me, gently led me away from there. She sat with me in silence until Prem came in.

'She's sleeping,' Prem said, his voice seeming to come from a long distance.

'Who?'

'Mriga. I've persuaded her parents to leave her here for a while. She refused to go back with them. I've given her something. She'll sleep for a few hours. Will you look after her, Manju? I've got to go out.'

I knew why and where. When Neeta left, I went to Mriga. She was in Sonu's room, I stayed there with her until she woke up. I didn't want her to be alone when she did. It was long past lunchtime when she came out of her drugged sleep. She opened her eyes, saw me and smiled. It was a happy smile. Then she looked round, realized where she was and the happiness vanished from her face. I moved to the bed and sat by her. She sat up, her arms clasped round her knees, her face young and tragic, and said, 'Can I stay here and not go home?'

'You're not going anywhere, Mriga.'

'I don't mean only for now, I mean for always.'

'I don't know, Mriga. Your mother may want you home.'

'Home!' she laughed. It was bitter laugh. Too adult for a

girl of her age. 'You don't know how it is. I'm a muddler, I'm stupid, I'm clumsy, I'm untidy, I'm slovenly. Are all parents like mine?' she asked naively.

'I don't know, Mriga. We try to do our best, but somewhere, somehow, we fail.'

I was speaking, not of her parents, but of myself; but she was too sunk in her own misery to take in what I was saying. 'I can't stay here, then?' she asked petulantly, a disappointed child.

'I don't know, Mriga,' I said again. 'I'll talk to your mother. If she agrees, you can.' But not for always, I wanted to say, but couldn't.

'My mother!' she said in scorn. 'Sometimes I talk to her rudely, I say things to her I really want to say to him. It's no fun, though. She's not real. She's only a shadow. His shadow. Sometimes I even feel sorry for her.' She sighed heavily. 'I can't even hate her properly.' She turned a puzzled face to me. 'Mothers are supposed to be important, aren't they? Mine isn't. I never even think of her.'

'Your father. . .' I was beginning when she interrupted me to say, 'I don't like him. Not any more.' She said it with the simple directness of a much younger child. 'At one time I used to dream, oh, all kinds of silly things. One of my favourite dreams was that I would be hurt in some kind of an accident, a car would run over me or something. And I would be lying in hospital, bandaged, you know, and pale and dying. And he would come to me. He would be terribly sorry. Tears would be pouring down his face. Mriga, Mriga, he would say. And I would smile bravely, and reply, Don't cry, Daddy and then I would die with a smile on my face and he would be heart-broken for ever and ever.' She smiled, a bitter, twisted smile. 'I've finished with such dreams now. I know he dislikes me.

And he lies. I heard him last night. He came home very late and I heard my mother asking him, Were you with her? And he said, Stop acting like an idiot. I told you I was held up in the hospital. That was a lie. I saw him with her.' She seemed to have forgotten that she had met me last night. 'Do you think she's beautiful?' she asked me abruptly. I knew who it was she meant.

'It depends,' I said feebly, not knowing what else to say

'I don't!' she said passionately. 'I think you're much prettier. You, or Meera Auntie, or Anand's mummy—or anyone! He has her photograph with him. I found it in his wallet. I took it out and burnt it. I thought, I'm burning her and she'll be dead. Now I know that even if she dies, he won't change. Sometimes I used to wish he would die, but now. . .' She shivered. 'I'm frightened, I'm frightened. Do you think he killed Guru Uncle? He hated him. I saw his face when he was talking to him. It scared me. And Tony Uncle. . .'

Her face took on an expression of horror; it came back to her, what she had seen in the morning. 'I went there in the morning. I thought I'll find something to show he was there, you know how people drop hankies and things like that in stories. I thought I'd show it to him and tell him, You lied, you're a liar. And then I saw was Tony Uncle. . .' She burst into tears.

I soothed and comforted her as well as I could, I made her eat something. She had a child's healthy appetite which asserted itself in spite of her ordeal of the morning. We were playing cards when Kamala came to tell us that Mriga's father had come to take her away. She clutched her cards to her chest and stared at me, her face terrified and blank. I went out to him, telling Mriga, 'You wait here. I'll talk to him.'

He listened to me, his face and body rigid with disapproval while I said my piece about Mriga wanting to stay on with me. He heard me with the utmost politeness, without interrupting me. Then he gave me a cold smile and said, 'It's very kind of you, but I wouldn't bother too much about what she says. I mean, you don't have to take her seriously. She's inclined to be rather hysterical and exaggerated at times, I'm afraid. And surely, you don't want any more trouble now, do you? I don't imagine either of you would like an awkward adolescent under your feet at such a time, would you? You've sent away your own little girl, haven't you?'

I could see, from the way he was emphasizing certain words, that he meant something unpleasant. I was overcome by anger, but I steadied myself. 'Dr Kulkarni, why don't you say it straight out, whatever you're trying to say? You don't have to hint and insinuate.'

Before he could reply, we heard a sound. There was Mriga leaning against the door in her peculiar boneless way. 'I'm ready,' she said to her father, 'let's go.'

He got up without another word and walked out. She followed him, then darted back to say to me, 'I must go. You understand, don't you?'

The appeal in her last words touched me. I nodded. She smiled at that, an adult smile. 'Thank you for having me,' she said, and she seemed to be parodying her father. Then the composure of her face gave way. 'Can I come again?'

'Any time,' I said.

I slept after that, feeling exhausted and drained. When I woke up, Kamala told me Prem had come and gone. I moved restlessly from room to room, not able to settle down to anything, not having the courage to find out, either, what was happening. I wondered whether I should go to Cynthia, but something held me back.

Cynthia herself came to me in the evening, when I was lying down. Kamala sent her straight up to me and she looked down at me with what looked like compassion. As if it was she who had come to comfort me. She looked serene, if a little paler. But I had a strange feeling that something had gone out of her, as if she was just a husk of herself.

'Where's Mriga?' she asked me.

'She's gone back home. Her father came for her and took her away. Come and sit down, Cynthia.'

She put her hand on my arm as I hoisted myself into a sitting position and asked me, 'And you? You're okay?'

'Perfectly fine,' I said.

She sat down suddenly, as if she had been drained of all her strength.

'Cynthia,' I said after a little silence, 'I don't know what to say. Except the usual thing—I'm sorry—and you know I mean it. Tony was. . .'

'The silly old fool!' she said with immense scorn and anger. 'The silly old fool.'

'Who?' I asked, astonished and perplexed.

'Tony!' The intensity of her anger showed her grief. 'Meddling in matters that were no business of his. You should have seen him at dinner last night. He was all cock-a-hoop. When he went out, he said, Don't wait for me. I've something to do. I may be late.'

'And did you stay up for him?' I asked, feeling sorry for her, imagining her waiting for a man who was, perhaps, already dead.

'I didn't know he hadn't come back. We occupy different rooms, you see.'

These few words explained much that had puzzled me
recently. And suddenly her mournful calm broke. 'He held it
against me that I didn't—I mean that I couldn't. . . Damn it,
you know what I'm saying. We'd stopped having sex. The truth
is, it made no sense to me, Manju. There were never going to
be any kids, see. Without that, it seemed just a selfish
indulgence. I had already sinned once, before marriage. Oh, I
was crazy about Tony then. There was still a year to go for my
finals and we were to get married only after that. Since we
were to be married, I thought, what's wrong? I should have
known. A wrong is a wrong. You can't escape the consequences.
When I realized that I was pregnant, I panicked. I took the
wrong way out. For a medical student, it wasn't very difficult to
do away with. . .' She hesitated and finally said, '. . .it. It didn't
seem a sin then, either. Just something that had to be done.
After all, we thought, we can have kids after we're married.
They never came. It was a punishment for what we had done.
We had sinned. And I had done something worse, I had taken
a life. I know this now. But Tony could never see it my way.'

She sighed, then said, 'Perhaps, it's better as it is. He'd been
going downhill ever since he lost his job. No, actually it began
even before that, though only God knows what drove him to
drinking the way he did. He always had an odd complex about
my being a doctor. If I'd given up my job and become a
pathetically clinging female, maybe things would have gone
right between us. Tony, poor man, was made to be a father,
the head of a family; without that role to play, he went to
pieces.'

She told me then that she would be going to Goa to meet
Tony's parents. 'How do you talk to a man, Manju, whose son
is dead? How does a mother feel to be told that? I should be

thankful, I sometimes think, that I'm not a mother. Tony's parents. . .' She smiled affectionately. 'To them, Tony was, still is, a celebrity. They have all his cups and shields in their parlour. My Tony—that's his mother's main topic of conversation. It was the only subject the two of us had in common. I wonder what we'll talk of now.' And then, once again, she spoke in a startling burst of fury, 'God, how I hate that man!'

'Who?' I asked, wondering if she meant Tony.

'Guru. If it hadn't been for him, we'd have gone on somehow. What business was it of his? Encouraging Tony to pour his woes into his ears, advising me, advising him—what had it to do with him? If only he hadn't come here. . .'

It was strange that I had to hear almost the same words once again that day. Neeta came late at night to see me. Prem was held up, she said, and had asked her to come and let me know that he would be late. Her face was pinched and haggard, she looked much older than her age. I thought she would go after giving me Prem's message, but she lingered. 'We're leaving, you know, Manju,' she said suddenly.

'And going where?'

'Shyam's resigning. He wants to go back to the States. He's always been hankering to go back. He never wanted to come here in any case. It was me—I was homesick, terribly homesick. I belong here, Manju, as I will never belong anywhere else. And there's Anand—I wanted my son to be brought up here, where he belongs. Where he's not a second-class citizen. As for Shyam, sometimes I wonder whether there's anything he cares about, apart from his work. There's no opportunity for research here, he says. What does that matter? Isn't it enough to help patients—that's what we're really trained for, aren't we?—and to do your work honestly and sincerely?'

'So you're going back,' I said thoughtfully, feeling very sorry somehow.

'What else can I do? Anand is so happy at the thought of going back. Can I stay here? Can I break up the family?' She made a gesture of helplessness that moved me deeply. 'There's my mother, I feel I'm abandoning her. She's old; it hurts terribly to leave her here and go. I wish,' her mouth became a grim line, 'I was like Shyam. Thinking of no one but myself. How much easier life would have been for me, if I had been made that way.' She gave me a crooked smile. 'But I can't blame anyone. I married him with my eyes open. I knew about him, I knew how hugely ambitious he was. I wanted him on any terms. No, I can't blame anyone. But Shyam blames Guru, he even said once that he hated him.'

I felt dazed and confused. And humble. Had I been totally wrong after all? Hadn't I known Guru at all? Had I made him into what I wanted him to be? As a girl, I'd dreamt of the perfect lover; as a young woman, of the perfect husband. For the past few years, it seemed to me now, I had been longing for the perfect friend. And I had thought I had found him in Guru. A man who understood and sympathized with all my feelings. It had been an almost perfect relationship, I thought. A woman would have known too much about my emotions and feelings; she would not have been as curious as Guru had been. With a man, of any age, there would have been that gritty, uneasy sense of our gender between us, we would have always been conscious of our sexual feelings. With Guru, maybe because of his illness, it had never been there.

But what was it that Guru had stirred up? And how had Tony died? Had he been killed too? Too? Was I admitting that Guru had been killed? But Tony? How had he died? I had not dared to ask Cynthia for any details, and Neeta had been listless and disinterested, absorbed in her own problems. I had to wait for Prem to come and tell me about Tony's death.

Suddenly I realized how late Prem was. Why was he so late? What could have happened? Each minute, as it ticked by, brought fresh horrors into my mind. I called Kamala and made her sit by my side. It had begun raining again, a steady downpour. Kamala's conversation was as soothing as the sound of the rain. We spoke of Sonu and I felt a pang of longing for my child. I'll get her back, I thought, as soon as all this is over. *This*? What was it? What was happening to us? When would it be over? And why was Prem so late?

Finally we heard the welcome sound of the gate being opened. 'Dada's come,' Kamala said, getting up hurriedly. 'Shall I put the food on the table?'

I waited until I heard the sound of the key being inserted in the latch. 'Yes, do that. We'll be ready in a few minutes.'

I went out into the hall. Prem was putting away his dripping umbrella. Then he sat down on the stool, staring at his hands. His face looked pinched and haggard. I felt sorry for him, but when I said, 'Prem,' he turned an imperturbable face to me. I hardened my heart. I could not go on, either. Finally it was he who spoke.

'Mriga?' he asked.

'Her father took her home.'

It seemed ages since Mriga had left me. I could scarcely believe it had just been a few hours ago.

'Is she all right?'

'I think so.'

'Oh!'

There was silence again. He began removing his shoes.

Angrily he wrenched them off his feet and dropped them with two separate thuds on the ground. He noticed me staring and asked, 'Are you all right?'

'I'm fine. But Tony?'

'Drowned, they say.' His voice was expressionless. 'They've taken his body for a post-mortem.' He sat silent again, hands loosely clasped between his legs, staring at his feet. There was something guarded about his face. Then abruptly he got up, kicking his shoes away from him. 'The funeral is tomorrow. Cynthia says she'd rather have it in Bombay. Tony and she have family there.'

Twelve

Another funeral. But this time, mercifully, distant from us. It was a horrible day, cheerless and gloomy. It was still raining, steady and monotonous. I had the horrors thinking of Tony being lowered into a flooded grave—like the man in Kipling's story—I remembered how the story had disturbed me. I stayed at home the whole morning. Tea, coffee, breakfast, lunch— that's how life goes on, I thought.

In the afternoon, there was a brief respite from the rain and I went out. The water ran down the gutters at the sides of the roads, carrying away, it seemed to me, all the debris of summer. A new term was beginning and I saw some freshers who must have just joined. They were unmistakable, with their unsoiled coats and their air of pride at having become medical students. I didn't know where to go and just roamed about aimlessly. Meera's house was locked. She'd never have gone anywhere without telling me about it, I thought. Somehow, the significance of that hurt. I shook off the thought.

Prem had not been home the night Tony died. He had cursed Tony. The damn fool, he had said, cursing Tony and banged out of the house. Oh no, not Prem. Anyone else, but not Prem. Surely, he would never hurt anyone, surely he could never hurt anyone. Or so I thought. How well did I know him, after all? I knew his body well enough, but his mind. . .?

'I'm glad I'm a pathologist,' he had said to me once. 'It's easier to deal with the dead. They can't feel, they don't suffer. I prefer the dead to living, suffering patients.'

But he had hated Guru. And he had cursed Tony. And there was Prabhakar Tambe—how did that name fit into this horrifying puzzle?

I was alone the whole day. It was as if I had been deliberately isolated. I welcomed it; my thoughts were not for sharing. In the evening, it began pouring again. The wind buffeted the house in an insane fury. The curtains flapped and beat maniacally. The rain was at its peak when Prem came in, looking like a drowned man. I heard him go up to change. I sat listlessly in the dining room. All kinds of odd, disconnected thoughts went through my mind. My students, ideas for a lecture, a book I'd recently read, Sonu, rains, mildew. . . It was as if I had to keep away thoughts of where Prem had been, of what he had gone to Bombay for.

'I met Sonu,' he said, coming in wiping his hands.

'Oh! How is she?'

He smiled. I had almost forgotten his smile and how attractive he looked when he smiled. 'Great! She wanted to come home with me. And when her granny said, You want to leave us and go, Sonu?, she said, I'll come back tomorrow, Ajji.'

We sat down to a silent dinner. The animation that had come upon his face when he spoke of Sonu had left it and he was sombre once again. It was a pretence of a meal, neither of us could eat. Finally I could bear it no more.

'Prem,' I said. 'talk to me, Prem. Please. I can't bear it any longer.'

He put down the glass of water he had been lifting and looked at me, so oddly that I had to brace myself to go on.

'Please,' I said desperately, 'let me talk to you. I can't be alone any more.'

His face flared into some intense feeling. 'You mean it, Manju? You want to talk to me?'

I had not seen him this way for long. So long. And then, he was doubtful and hesitant once again. He asked me, 'You mean it?'

'Yes, yes, yes!' I said, as emphatically as I could. 'I just can't go on this way any more.'

'Nor can I, Manju, nor can I!' He took my hands and held them so tightly that I winced with pain. 'Today, watching Tony lying there, I felt as if nothing would ever be the same. If it hadn't been for me, would Tony have died?'

He was saying them now, the words I had so feared, the words I had not dared to utter even to myself, but somehow they didn't frighten me any more. Instead, there was relief. Would he have said them, and said them so sorrowfully, if he had done something wrong?

'Tony was killed, wasn't he?'

'Yes.'

'Like Guru was?'

'Yes, I believe that too, now. I know it now, Manju. I know that maybe I'm hurting you by saying this, but I must. If Guru hadn't—I mean, it was his fault. He was either a malicious man, or a silly fool. Or even, maybe, like you thought him, a saint. I don't know which is true. Possibly he was all of these. But it was his fault, all right.'

'You forget,' I said. 'I know nothing of what Guru did. Only that he was kind to me.'

'And I wasn't?' Prem flashed at me. I said nothing. 'Maybe I wasn't. But you were so aloof, so withdrawn, so encased in your armour of righteousness, how could I tell you what I had done?'

It was as if the pieces were falling into place at last. 'It was Prabhakar Tambe, wasn't it?'

'Yes, it began with him. You know about it, Manju?'

I shook my head. 'Only that he was a labour union leader. And he died in hospital.'

'If it was only that!' he smiled, a bitter smile. 'He came to us with a problem. Acute intestinal obstruction, cause not known—that was Kulkarni's diagnosis. They decided to do an exploratory laparotomy and then deal with the obstruction. Shyam was going to do the surgery. A simple matter really, for a surgeon like him. But for some reason, when he was exploring—there were multiple adhesions—he accidentally cut through a major vessel. Shyam, who was so meticulous, such a wonderfully careful surgeon, to do such a thing! Everyone there must have been stupefied. The patient, sorry, I mean Tambe, began to bleed. Even before they could think of doing anything, there was a rapid fall of BP, he had a cardiac arrest and was gone.'

'And then?' I prompted him. He seemed to find it difficult to go on.

'It's so difficult to explain now, Manju. Sometimes one just can't understand how things happen. Maybe Kulkarni didn't do a detailed cardiac work-up. Actually, he left it to the resident; later we realized that the girl had made some queries which should have been followed up by Kulkarni, he should have rechecked some of the findings. But he didn't. And maybe Shyam was too casual, as well. It was a very simple problem, you see. Nothing difficult or unusual about it. You know how we crave for unusual cases, so that we can write up a paper on it later.' His voice was bitter. 'Actually, Shyam could have safely left the surgery to a junior. There's Stephen, he's sufficiently competent. If only he had! But Tambe was a kind of VIP, you know, Shyam had to do it himself. And so Tambe died on the operation table.'

'Oh my God!'

'If they'd done a full cardiac check-up, they would have realized there was a risk. If they had been more careful, perhaps, he wouldn't have died. Complacency—that's the only explanation that occurs to me.'

I thought of Tony's voice saying, Complacent bastards!

'It was inexcusable. Plain, simple negligence, really. Not that it never happens. It happens, it's happened many times, more often than patients realize. Doctors are only human and they can also make mistakes. But here it was different. A man died. That was bad enough. But worse, that man happened to be Tambe. I don't know if you have any idea of the hold Tambe had on the workers. He was a union leader because of his intimate contact with the workers. He never put on airs about being a union leader, he remained a worker, one of them. He was a rare man, a man in a million. And so, Tambe being who he was and what he was, there was a huge crowd waiting outside the hospital while he was being operated. Shyam panicked. All of them went into a blue funk. They called the Dean. And he came to me later '

I knew now what was coming. But I waited for Prem to say it. We had waited for this moment too long, both of us.

'You can imagine what they wanted me to do. The Dean as good as told me I had no choice. It was not a threat. Oh no! You know he's incapable of that. But I would be destroying so much, he said. And the man was dead, anyway; nothing would bring him back, he said. Such a specious argument, but used so often. The Dean said that all that I had to do was to falsify the cause of death in my autopsy report. Give the surgeon a clean chit.'

Seeing my face, Prem said gently, 'Don't blame the Dean too much, Manju. The management was after him. Tambe was a leader of the workers in the Sethji's mill. God knows what would have happened if the truth had leaked out. And the Dean was not thinking of himself as much as he was of the hospital. I know that.'

'And Guru?'

'Guru.' For the first time Prem smiled. 'What had he to do with all this? I wonder myself. Nothing really. And yet, as it turns out now, everything. I don't know how, when and where he first came to know about this. Obviously, someone told him. Maybe Ashok just casually mentioned Tambe and his unfortunate death. There were others in the OT, like the theatre sister, who certainly knew the truth. Perhaps someone spoke to Guru about it. You know how he could get people to talk. Anyway, Guru started to probe. And then he began to work on people. He started with Kulkarni. He didn't get anywhere with him, I imagine. He went to Shyam too, I suppose. I was on his list as well. My God, he was naïve, that fellow! He had met Tambe's wife, widow, rather.' Prem's face twitched. 'And he asked me, Have you people any idea of what you've done? He told me about the kind of work Tambe had been doing among the workers. And about his widow. Tara, he called her, as if he knew her well. God, he knew how to get to you, all right. He told me, I remember, of Tambe's three children. One of them, the eldest, a daughter, was very bright and appearing for her SSC this year. And there were two younger boys in school. The management had given them a lump sum as compensation, they had given the wife a job and promised the daughter one when she wanted it. But for Guru that was not enough. Reparation—that was what Guru wanted. Money, he said to me, is no compensation to a woman who's lost her husband, to kids who've lost their father, money, he said, is not enough. But, he told me, you can make things right with yourself. At times,' and now Prem's smile was one of genuine amusement, 'it seemed to me he was repeating something he'd read somewhere. In fact, he mentioned *Crime and Punishment* to me, he spoke of the girl who advises Raskolnikov to beg for God's forgiveness for having murdered the old woman. I read the book myself after he spoke of it. Remember how surprised you were to see me reading it? It was because of Guru. I wondered what he saw himself as. A Jesus Christ? A Gandhi? No, I don't want to be harsh. He was sincere, he did think we could do something to right the wrong. Perhaps it's not Guru who was crazy, but *we* who were hard and callous. Tambe was a man, not merely a patient. We should have thought of him as a man who died when he needn't have, not just an unfortunate mishap that happened in the theatre. A figure in the hospital statistics. Anyway, I was talking about Guru. He wanted us to come out with the truth. I don't know what he said to Shyam and Kulkarni, but as for me, he held the threat of telling you about it over me.'

'And why didn't you tell me about it yourself?'

'How could I? You were so—so bloody honest, so. . .so much against doing anything wrong, I was afraid you would turn away from me. I thought you would despise me. I should have been a strong, virtuous hero, refusing to knuckle under. Instead. . . I thought you didn't care about me, anyway. That you had never cared. You married me because, well, because you had to marry someone. You had told me about Rajiv, remember?'

'No, no, Prem,' I stammered, eager to convince him, desperate to make him understand, furious that I couldn't get the right words fast enough. 'It isn't true now. Maybe at that time—no, not even then. To tell you the truth, I don't know what I felt then. Now that girl seems to be another person, not me at all. What is Rajiv compared to the life we have together? To the kind of life we can build together with our children? I was a damn fool, Prem. I thought I was doing the right thing, the honest thing, by telling you about it. But I was stupid, I never thought that I would be hurting you. I was just proud of my honesty. Rajiv. . .' I smiled. A shadow now. A ghost. No, not even that. A mirage. 'He doesn't exist any more. There's only you. And Sonu. And this baby waiting to be born.'

There was a storm raging outside. Guru, who had been my friend, was dead. And Tony lay in his newly-dug grave, with the rain beating on him, while Cynthia grieved her heart out in angry sorrow by herself. But within me, there was peace. I was no longer alone.

We sat in silence for a long while, a silence that was companionable. We had long since abandoned the farce of eating a meal. Kamala had cleared up and gone to bed.

'Shall I go on?' Prem asked me.

I nodded.

'Guru was working on the Dean, too. You know how the Dean admired Guru. I think he was weakening. He was thinking of letting the truth emerge, thinking of resigning. But there were the rest of us, Shyam, Kulkarni, the anaesthetist Pawar and I. Pawar has left, but the rest of us had to be considered.

The Dean was not alone in what he had done; he had to consult us. He talked to me about it. I felt—to tell you the truth, I don't know what I felt. Scared, maybe. Perhaps, relieved as well. I had never been happy about our cover-up. And then Guru died.'

'Murdered, Tony said. He told me about it, the evening he died. I never told you about that, did I?'

'No, you didn't. What did he say, Manju?' Prem leaned forwards eagerly. I searched my mind, trying to remember what it was that Tony had told me. Only two days ago, yet it seemed years, decades back.

'Think, Manju,' Prem urged me when I paused. 'It matters. You've got to remember.'

And then I did. Tony's words came back to me.

Tony had spoken of the evening before Guru's death. 'I was a bit sozzled, remember?' he had said with a wry smile. 'Ashok had taken me to lie down, as if I'd been a naughty boy who had to be punished.'

He lay there, he told me, suddenly sober, aware of what he had done, dreading the thought of going home and facing Cynthia. He couldn't bear, he admitted, to see her face— disappointed in him, ashamed of him.

Then he'd heard footsteps in the corridor, the sound of a door opening and closing. He knew it was Guru's room and when he heard the footsteps going away, he decided to visit Guru. 'He was the only one I felt comfortable with. And there he was, lying alone,' he'd said.

Guru was awake, but his voice was thick, his words slurred. Tony guessed they'd given him something to make him sleep, he thought he'd go away. But Guru had asked him to stay. He was just a bit groggy, Guru had said. He'd had two pricks instead of one, he told Tony; maybe one is no longer enough, he had said.

So Tony stayed. After a while Guru fell asleep and Tony went out. Later, after Guru's death, he'd spoken to Ashok about it and Ashok had been shocked. He said no one was supposed to give Guru any injections except himself. And Ashok had already given him his usual dose of pethidine that evening.

I stopped at that. Prem took a deep breath as if he'd been holding it all this while and said, 'Pethidine? Easy enough to give another big dose. Guru would have taken it from any one of us.'

'And Tony? How did he die? Maybe he was drowned after all.'

Prem looked at me with pity. 'Drowned? Of course he was drowned. Narvekar told me there was water in his lungs. But it couldn't have been an accident. How is it possible for a man of Tony's size to drown in a puddle like that? The water was nowhere deeper than four feet.'

'Narvekar? You mean you didn't do the post-mortem?'

'I couldn't, Manju. I know we doctors pride ourselves on our ability to be detached. But how could I cut Tony up?' He was silent for a moment, then went on, 'No, it couldn't have been an accident. The only other possibility is that, perhaps, he was drunk.'

'No, he wasn't. Not when I met him, anyway. He was perfectly sober. And later, Cynthia and he had dinner together. She said he was all right then, too.'

'Well, I hope the chemical analysis will tell us something about that. But Narvekar told me that Tony had a large bruise on his head. And his fingers, they were—they looked as if he had been scrabbling for a hold, and someone had forcibly made him let go. His nails were broken, torn off, the fingertips smashed. It doesn't bear thinking of. Ever since Narvekar told me this, I keep thinking of Tony trying to get out of the water and someone hitting him on his hands to loosen his grip, holding his head down in the water. . .'

'Oh my God! Who, Prem? Who could do that?'

'I wish we knew. Or, maybe I wish we never will. No, that's wrong, it'll make us all suspicious of one another, we won't be able to work together ever again.'

'Prem. . .' I said in a small voice, remembering something.

'What?'

'Mriga told me something yesterday morning. I think you ought to know.'

And I told him about Kulkarni and Rani Agarwal, and of how I had come across Mriga in a hysterical state that evening. 'She says that when she left me she didn't go back home. Not at once. She had some funny idea of waiting for her father, of confronting him with what she had seen. She waited on a bench near the tennis court. But her father never came that way. Someone else did. Two people. Tony and the Dean.'

We stared at each other in silence. Then I went on. 'He's not the only one, Prem. Cynthia hated Guru. She told me so herself. And Vimala. And that woman of Ashok's. She was in Ashok's house that evening.'

Prem removed his glasses and wiped his eyes, like a weary child. His hand groped for mine and held on to it as if it was his only hope.

'Let's leave it there, shall we? That's enough for now. I can't take it any more. Honestly, I can't. Let's just leave it for tonight.'

We left it there. We didn't talk of Guru and his death any more. But that was all the respite we were to have. Well, at least we had that. And, how strange, that night before going to bed, I read an old favourite by Agatha Christie. When I finished reading, I put the book away, switched off the light and thought of what was happening to us, to all of us. And I thought how bizarre it was that murder, a word which had belonged between the covers of a book, had insinuated itself into our lives.

Thirteen

Early next morning, there was a phone call for Prem. The conversation was brief, with only monosyllabic answers on Prem's part. When Prem came back, his face was bleak.

'That was Narvekar. He wanted to know whether he can give the autopsy report to the police.'

'And?' I asked apprehensively.

'I told him to go ahead. Now it will become a case of murder.'

For an instant I had a vision of Tony as he had been, and I was filled with rage. Murder was not just a frightening word any more. It was hateful, a cruel rejection of a man's humanity, of his right to live.

'The injuries make it clear that he was pushed into the tank and held down in the water. But we have to wait for the chemical analyser's report to get an idea of whether Tony was drunk—or drugged.'

'What next?' I asked Prem.

'I suppose I have to inform the Dean about this.'

He began to button up his shirt as he walked back to the phone. Some instinct made me stop him just as he picked up the phone.

'Prem,' I said, 'don't talk about this on the phone. Call him here and tell him.'

He looked at me for a while, realization and understanding dawning in his eyes. Then he nodded. 'He'll be here in a few minutes,' he said putting the phone down.

'Breakfast?' I asked.

'Let's wait.'

Prem prowled around restlessly while he waited for the Dean. The few minutes stretched out and it was almost half an hour before the Dean opened the gate and walked briskly in.

'Prem?' he asked me.

'He's waiting for you.'

He went in without saying anything more. I sat in the hall with the newspaper in my hands; but I was not reading it, I was just looking at the words. Waiting for the Dean and Prem to finish their talk. In a while, the Dean came out alone. The man who went in had been brisk and purposeful. This one walked like an old man, with slow, lagging steps, his shoulders bowed, eyes fixed on the ground. He passed me by unseeingly. I thought he would go without saying a word to me. But when he reached the door, he suddenly halted, as if he had thought of something, and came back slowly to me.

'You know, Manju,' he said, speaking as if he was thinking aloud, 'I've just realized something. It's strange, but I never really thought of Tony at all. Oh yes, I knew him well. He was Tony D'Mello, a good fellow. Someone to talk to and laugh with when we met. But the truth is that, to me, he was only Cynthia's husband.'

'He can be Cynthia's husband. That's good enough for him'—hadn't Tony said that himself?

'Cynthia was important to me, you know, because she worked in the hospital. A very good paediatrician. While Tony was only Cynthia's husband. Beyond that, he meant nothing at all.' He went on reflectively, tracing patterns in the dust on the table. No, not patterns; it was his initials, RA, that he was writing, over and over again, the two letters entwined together.

'Humans, we don't think of them enough. Ideas, principles, ideology, ambitions, success—so many other things come first. And there's our own ego—that heads the list of what matters to us. But it's wrong. It's people who matter most. Nothing should matter more than them.'

He raised his eyes now, as if he was looking at something. And as if I had been vouchsafed a glimpse into his mind, I knew what it was he was seeing. The hospital. And I remembered how he had sent his children away to a boarding school at an early age, because there had been no school here in those days. And how, we had heard, Rani had violently protested at first, and finally drifted away herself. So he has them too, I thought, moments of self-flagellation, when you feel everything you've done is wrong.

Meanwhile the Dean went on, scarcely conscious, I began to realize, that I was there. He was talking to himself. 'I wanted to do good,' he said, 'I wanted to do something to make people's lives better. But along the way, I came to understand that you can't do anything unless you have power. And now I know what power is. You imagine that because you are doing good, you have the right to do anything. Yes, power is like a strong dye. It colours you, it can be lethal.'

He paused again. 'So many wrongs,' he said, softly, after a little while. 'If I had my life again. . . No, I'm not sure I'd have done things differently. But Guru made me realize that you can undo your wrongs. It's not difficult. It's never too late, no, never too late.'

And then he walked away, abruptly, purposefully, as if he had come to some decision.

Prem left a little later. 'I'm late,' he mumbled. 'We have a Death Conference at eight.'

Suddenly I shivered. How close they were to death, these doctors, how intimate they were with it! Didn't it make them indifferent to it? Once again I was alone at home. The previous day, I had suffered a feeling of loneliness, of isolation. Today, it was different. After our talk, Prem's and mine, I knew I was not alone. Nevertheless, I felt surrounded by menacing shapes. Shapes that had faces and names I knew. But somehow, they were suddenly strangers to me. Which one of them could have killed two people? It could be any one of them. It was a terrifying thought. I went over the facts and the names over and over again. However many times I did it, it never made any sense. And yet the fact remained: two people had died and one of us was responsible for it.

Prem rang me up some time in the afternoon, 'Have your lunch,' he said, 'I can't get away. I'm not sure what time I can come home.'

A little later the doorbell rang. I started up in apprehension. Then I heard Vidya's clear voice and relaxed. There was something about her calmness and composure that was soothing and brought me back to sanity. I relegated my fears to the back of my mind.

'I've brought you your capsules,' she said. 'Gautam told me he'd promised you he'd get them for you.'

'Oh, thanks,' I said. 'You shouldn't have bothered. Prem would have picked them up from Gautam.'

'Gautam would have come himself, but it's his outpatient today. The poor man is inundated with women. No wonder he dislikes women!'

'Gautam does?' I asked in surprise.

'Didn't you ever guess?' She smiled, but didn't go on. She said instead, 'Oh yes, the reason why I came to you myself is that I wanted to speak to Mriga.'

'Mriga? She isn't here, she's in her own home.'

'But her father said. . .'

'No, she went away the same day. Her father took her home.'

'Then why did he say she was here?' She chewed her lips thoughtfully. 'He distinctly said she's here.'

'I can't imagine why he did! As a matter of fact, I haven't seen her since then.'

'Oh well, Dr Kulkarni is a strange man. For all his polite, smooth exterior, he's really a turbulent character. He can't bear any disagreement, no, none at all. Any opposition throws him off balance. If you disagree with him, he takes it as a personal insult. He's the same in our conferences and meetings, it's painful to see a man with such a thin skin.'

'I dislike him,' I said bluntly. 'What he's doing to Mriga is inexcusable.'

'I know. I'm worried about her,' she said.

'Anyway, she's back home now.'

'Well, yes, but. . .' It seemed as if she would say something more. Instead, she deliberately changed the subject. 'Ram was here this morning, wasn't he? He told me about it.'

'Yes. Tony now—it's unbelievable, isn't it, that one of us could do such a thing. I mean, who?'

'I don't know, Manju. Could be anyone. I'd rather not guess. All this talk and mud-slinging that's going around seems pretty senseless to me. I don't know why people can't just do their work and not get into things that don't really concern them.'

She sounded like a school teacher disapproving of some silly activity. As if she was saying, Murder! What a waste of time! Come on, children, back to work. I began to laugh.

'What's the matter?' she asked me in surprise.

'Nothing. Just a thought.'

'Oh! Well, I must go. Lunch, then back to work. Look after yourself. And. . .' it came out with a hesitancy that was very unlike Vidya, 'why don't you invite Mriga to your place for a few days? It's. . .' Again she hesitated and then came out with 'better', a word which I somehow knew was not what she had really meant to say.

My uneasiness increased after she had gone. It was a joke that the Gynaec Department was the last to hear any news, with both Gautam and Vidya being disinclined to gossip or to listen to gossip. And now Vidya, Vidya, who wouldn't gossip, Vidya who wouldn't talk scandal, had tried to tell me something. Gautam, she had said, dislikes women. What did that mean? Had she meant what I thought she had meant? Somebody else too had said something about Gautam once. What was it? And who had said it? It evaded me. And Mriga. 'She's at home now,' I had said. 'Yes, but. . .' She had left that sentence incomplete. But what? And then her last words: 'Why don't you invite Mriga home for a few days?'

Dr Kulkarni. He had hated Guru. He had been out that night, not very far from where Tony had been. He had been in Ashok's house the evening Guru died. On an impulse, I picked up the phone and dialled the Kulkarnis' number. I could hear it ringing. I held on for a long time, but no one picked it up, it just went on ringing. There was something ominous about the sound, about the silence surrounding it. Finally, I put the receiver down and dialled Neeta's number. The phone was instantly picked up.

'Anand?' I asked.

'Yeah, it's me.'

'Look, can you do me a favour?'

'Sure.'

'Can you find out if Mriga's at home?'

'She's there all right. I saw her in her room some time ago. She looked a bit sick, I thought. Do you want me to get her?'

'No,' I said slowly. 'Leave it. Thanks a lot.'

But it was not easy to leave it at that. I had to see Mriga. I would go there myself.

Shanta opened the door and stood in silence, waiting for me to explain my presence. She made no pretence of welcoming me in, or of giving me a polite smile.

'Is Mriga at home?' I asked. I was slightly breathless. I had hurried, urged by God-knows-what reason.

'Yes, she's here.'

'Can I talk to her? I'm all alone at home, you see, and I thought I'd take her back with me for company,' I tried to explain myself in some way, knowing I sounded awkward and uncertain.

'She's not well. She's sleeping.'

'Oh?'

There seemed to be nothing more to say. And then, a sudden change came over Shanta. It was not that she smiled or looked friendly, but it was as if she had understood my anxiety and was responding to it.

'She's all right,' she said to me. 'I'm looking after her. She'll be all right.'

There was nothing to do after that, but to go away. 'I'm looking after her,' Shanta had said. Was that a reassurance? But Dr Kulkarni? Nonsense, no father, however unnatural, would harm his daughter. It was a wild idea, anyway.

But my fears wouldn't leave me. I waited impatiently for Prem to come home, so that I could share them with him. Prem himself rang me up a little later. 'Manju,' he asked me abruptly, 'have you seen the Dean?'

'Yes, of course. He was here in the morning, wasn't he?'

'No, I mean after that.'

'No, I haven't seen him after that. Is anything wrong?'

'Don't know. I hope not. Don't worry, anyway. I'll be back soon.'

He returned with furrows of anxiety on his face. 'I haven't been able to trace him. Nobody has seen him today. His secretary knows nothing, nor do Rani and Vidya. They don't seem to think that there's anything unusual about his absence, but I'm afraid, Manju. He was in a strange mood when he left me in the morning. Nobody has seen him after that. Did he say anything to you?'

I told him about our conversation—well, not a conversation, actually, it had been a monologue of the Dean's, actually. Prem's expression was even more troubled when I finished. 'I don't like it, Manju. I don't like it at all.'

He was miserably restless. Though he had eaten nothing since morning, he said he didn't want lunch. 'Just give me a cup of tea,' he said. After he'd drunk his tea, he got up with resolution. It was as if he had made up his mind. 'I'm going out,' he told me. 'I can't sit here just waiting. Do you mind?'

I shook my head. 'Where are you going?'

'To Shyam first. Maybe he knows something. After that. . .? I don't know. I'll see. Don't worry too much about me—or about anything. I'll be back as soon as I can.' Suddenly, when leaving, he said, 'Don't stay alone at home. Go to Meera's.'

'I am all right,' I reassured him. 'Kamala's with me.'

But Kamala was to go out that evening. There was the usual weekly movie in the recreation hall, and I had promised Kamala she could go. She often did, with a family she had made friends with. She offered to stay with me, but I didn't have the heart to deprive her of her treat.

The house was horribly silent after she left and I regretted my decision to stay alone. Should I go to Meera's house? But Meera and Ashok had looked askance at Prem (or had I, perhaps, imagined it?) and the thought hurt. Surely there should be trust among friends? Then I thought again of what Vidya had said. 'Could be anyone,' she had said. Yes, that was true. There was that girl—woman, rather—Ashok had got involved with. Tony had seen her in Ashok's house the day Guru died. Ashok had admitted to her presence. When Tony had spoken of her in the club, Ashok had looked at him as if he could kill him. But surely, Ashok couldn't have killed Guru? Why, he was the one who first brought up the idea of something suspicious about Guru's death. Why would he have done that if he himself had been the killer? Or was that a strategy to divert suspicion?

And Gautam—yes, I remembered now, it was Guru who had said something about him. He had hinted that he was not a good man. What had he meant by that? Gautam had hated Guru all right. And I always felt that, behind that casual exterior of Gautam's, there was a streak of ruthlessness. What about the Dean? What if Guru had threatened his beloved hospital? And what was it he had said this morning, something about undoing wrongs? Then there were the Shahs. . .

I found myself getting more and more muddled and confused. This was not just an interesting puzzle, a whodunnit I was reading; these were real people, people I knew. I just could not associate them with murder. And yet, motives lay about thickly, there was certainly no dearth of them.

The phone rang, startling me out of my thoughts. I walked as fast as I could to pick it up. It was Rani.

'Manju,' she said and her voice sounded quite different, as if she had been crying. There was no artifice in it any more. 'Is Prem at home?' she asked

'No, he's just gone out. Has the Dean come back?'

'No, not yet.' There was an attempt to be casual, but Rani gave it up the next moment, saying in a breathless voice, 'It's Ram. Where do you think he could have gone, Manju? I'm frightened.'

'Prem is trying to find out where the Dean is. I'll ask him to ring you up as soon as he returns. Or shall I ask him to see you?'

To my bewilderment, she suddenly switched once again to her pose of assumed indifference. 'No, no, don't bother,' she said. And, before I could say any more, she put the phone down. I put the receiver down myself, gently, carefully, and stared at it as if it could answer the questions in my mind. Suddenly I got up. I wouldn't sit here and brood any longer. I'd go to Rani. Surely, there had been something she had tried to convey to me. What had it been? Fear? Yes, that was the message that had come to me across the wire. Rani was scared. I had to go to her.

It was getting harder and harder for me to walk with any comfort, but it felt better to be out, to be walking, to be doing something. I hesitated for a moment outside the Dean's door, feeling an intruder. Then Rani's words, her voice, came back to me: 'Manju, I'm frightened.' Firmly I rang the bell. Nathu opened the door. When I asked for Rani, he just pointed towards the drawing room. I went in. The curtains were drawn, and the room was dark, only a single light in a far corner of the room fighting the darkness. Rani sat on a sofa, looking like a beautiful butterfly pinned to a grey board. She stared at me with dull, uncomprehending eyes.

'Rani,' I ventured. She said nothing, she didn't even look at me.

I gently put out my hand and touched her wrist on which her gaudy glass bangles glittered and sparkled. At my touch, I could feel her slowly registering my presence. She gave me a curious half-seeing look, then opened her eyes and said, 'Manju?'

'Is anything wrong?'

She made a peculiar grimace and asked, 'Wrong?' She repeated the word like a child stalling for time.

'The Dean—Prem is worried about him. Where is he? Isn't he home?'

'He's all right,' she spoke petulantly, as if she had forgotten that she had said, 'I am frightened' to me just a short while ago. 'Why should Prem worry?' And then, without warning, she flung herself off the sofa and sat on the floor, her face buried in her arms, her body shaking and heaving as she gave way to sobs. I could do nothing but offer her the comfort of my presence if she wanted it. I looked down at her and noted in faint surprise that she was going grey, something I had never noticed before.

At last the sobs slowed down, became fainter. Her body stopped heaving. She climbed back on the sofa, clumsily, very unlike her usual graceful movements, and blew her nose loudly. It was an almost fierce honk.

'The Dean. . .?' I began, after a pause.

But she went back to what she'd said before, as if her tears were an interlude to be ignored. 'He's all right,' she said. 'He'll be back soon. He's just gone out.'

'Are you all right?'

'Yes, I'm fine.'

Suddenly she seemed eager to be rid of me. I had no option but to get up. As I did, she got up too and slipped her feet back into her heeled sandals. Now she was taller than I was. As if this brought back her self-confidence, she looked at me in her usual, superior, 'I'm the Dean's wife' manner. 'Can you go back by yourself?' she asked me kindly. 'Shall I ask the driver to drop you back?'

'Of course not. Walking is good for me.'

I looked back once and saw her standing there in the middle of the room, a confused look on her face. The house was silent. Was it always like this? I felt fleeting pity for Rani. No wonder she preferred not to be here. I wondered where Vidya was.

I was just opening the front door to let myself out, when Rani came to me in a rush. She clutched my arm in a tight, hurting grip and said, 'Manju, don't go. Don't leave me here alone. I can't bear it. I'm scared.'

'What is it?' I asked fearfully.

'It's Ram. He went out early in the morning. After he came back, he got a phone call. Then he came to me.' Her lips trembled. 'He said that he had received a call, that the person told him something about me. He asked me whether it was true. And I said. . .' She raised her head defiantly, as if enacting that scene for me. 'I said it was not true. And he said, Don't lie to me, don't ever lie to me. And I said no, I was not lying. Then he went mad. Lies, lies, all lies, he began to yell. He'd never shouted at me that way before.' Rani's eyes had the bewildered look of a beloved child who had been rebuked for the first time. 'He said that he was tired of it all, he said he'd like to blow it all up. I didn't know what he was saying, I couldn't understand him. He didn't explain anything, he just rushed away. And he hasn't come back as yet. Manju, what do you think has happened to him?'

I wondered what shape her fears were taking. Obviously someone had told the Dean about her affair with Dr Kulkarni. What did she think the Dean would do now? Commit suicide? Divorce her? Kill Dr Kulkarni? It would be just like Rani, I thought, to make up tragic scenes, with herself as the heroine of the story. But no, it wasn't funny any longer. Her face was tragic.

I did not tell her my own fears, that the Dean had, perhaps, gone to a rendezvous with the killer. She had enough to cope with—repentance, shame, guilt—without having to cope with the extra burden of fear.

'You won't go? You'll stay with me?'

I stayed with her. We went back into the drawing room and sat there, waiting for what we scarcely knew ourselves. The Dean's footsteps in the hall? His voice saying, Sorry, I'm late?

The phone rang once. Rani looked at me, making no move to get up. I picked it up, it was Shyam. He showed no surprise on hearing my voice. 'Has he returned?' he asked, without any preamble.

'No.'

There was a pause. 'Okay, I'll come over.'

In a few minutes he was with us, he, Neeta, and Prem, whom they had met at the gate.

'Rani,' Prem said, going straight to her, 'he's nowhere.

We've tried all the possible places. Do you know any place where he could be?'

She hadn't moved when they all came in. She sat there listlessly, unconcerned about anything but her own fears, her own misery.

'Any place?' she said vaguely. 'I don't know. I can't think.'

'Where's Vidya?'

'I don't know.' It came out a pathetic wail.

'She's at the hospital,' Neeta said. 'We met her, Mama and I, a little while back. She said there was a patient she had to see.'

'Did she say anything about the Dean?'

'No.'

'Look,' Shyam butted in impatiently, speaking for the first time, 'what's the point delaying any more? We've got to do something. It's no use just sitting here and waiting.'

'What can we do?' I asked.

'First thing,' Prem set his lips in a grim line, 'I'm going to speak to the others, ask them if they know something. Mind if I use the phone, Rani?'

'What?' Rani looked vaguely at him.

'The phone? Can I use it?'

She made a gesture which Prem interpreted as 'go ahead,' and he began to dial.

Fourteen

I will never forget that night, not for as long as I live. Do I believe in ghosts? Yes, perhaps I do, for that night it was as if Guru and Tony were with us through all the hours that we were gathered there. Guru and Tony, who were dead—and I could feel their presence around us. It was we, all of us, who looked like ghosts, actually. Yes, we were all there. Prem had rung them up, telling them of the Dean's disappearance and soon they were with us, awkward and shocked. But, no, surely not all of us felt that way? Surely, one of us was cautious, wary, wondering whether his (her?) secret was safe?

Ostensibly, there was only sympathy and concern on all our faces; yet the fear in the room made itself felt. There was a feeling of tension in the room that didn't come from fear for the Dean alone, and an awareness of this tension in every averted glance, in every faltering look. Gautam was the only one who didn't seem to be affected. He sat by Rani, who had sunk into apathy, and looked just as usual, except that he ruffled his hair more often. And his face had lost its usual casual look, the look of good-natured indifference that was part of his charm. Now he seemed disinterested in what was happening around him; strangely, this seemed to me close to cruelty. Guru's words about Gautam came back to me. 'It's not enough for a man to be skilful,' he had said. 'He's got to be a good human being as well.' And when I had asked him to explain, he had said something about being unable to reveal other people's secrets. What was Gautam's secret? Had Guru ferreted it out, as he had so many others? I thought of how jealously Gautam guarded his reserve, his private life, and wondered whether he would have any compunction getting rid of the person who threatened that reserve.

And then it came to me too, the same thought so many of us had expressed: why couldn't Guru have left us alone? What were we, after all, but men and women like so many others, made up of many parts, some good, some bad? Perhaps the evil in us would have lain dormant if Guru hadn't stirred things up and brought it to the surface. But then, there was Prabhakar Tambe. . .

Dr Kulkarni, the man who fascinated me most, sat far away from Rani. He hadn't looked at her once since he came in. She had, however, given him one scared look, then subsided into her apathy once again. Dr Kulkarni, I thought, looked definitely frightened. He made no pretence of being otherwise. This man, I knew, had a streak of cruelty in him. And he had two possible motives. Shanta sat by him. She had smiled at me when she entered. It was almost cataclysmic, a smile from her. There had been something diffident about the smile that had reminded me of Mriga.

'Is Mriga alone at home?' I had asked her.

'No, she's with Neeta's mother. Anand and she are playing chess.'

'Shanta. . .' her husband said, touching her on the arm, as if warning her. She looked at him, and there was, I thought, a touch of defiance about the look. Suddenly it occurred to me that it must have been Shanta who had rung up the Dean about Rani and her husband. Yes, for some reason, I was convinced that it was her. It wasn't just surmise. I *knew.* The worm turning at last?

There was no pretence of conversation among us. We sat as still and silent as ghosts. It was on this scene that Vidya walked in.

'What the. . .!' she exclaimed, on seeing all of us.

She switched on the lights and we blinked in the strong light. Vidya seemed flabbergasted to see so many people in the room. She was still wearing her white coat, her hands, balled into fists, thrust deep into her pockets, as if she was supporting herself on them.

'What's going on here?' She looked at everyone, and then turned an enquiring gaze on Rani, who continued to gaze dully in front of her.

'Have I gatecrashed into a party I know nothing about?'

'Have you only just come home, Vidya?' Gautam asked her.

'Yes, you know I was busy with a C section. But what's going on here?' Her voice rose impatiently on the last word.

'It is the Dean,' Ashok replied.

'Ram? What about him?'

Now she seemed shaken. Her hand went up to her throat in a rather theatrical gesture, but there was no mistaking the anxiety on her face.

'Have you seen him, Vidya?' Rani sat up eagerly, as if she had only just seen Vidya.

'Ram? Yes, of course.'

'When?' Shyam pounced on her.

Vidya's head swivelled on her neck as she turned to him from Rani. Her eyes had that cold. 'What business is it of yours?' look. But they faltered before Shyam's steady stare.

'Early morning, actually; we had our morning tea together. He told me he was going to see Prem after his bath. I saw him again a little later, walking to the car park. He seemed to be in a hurry.' She paused, as if expecting someone to say something. When the silence continued, she went on, 'Will someone tell me what's wrong?'

This was the real Vidya hidden behind the façade of the cool professional woman. She looked terrified.

'Let's hope there's nothing wrong. But the Dean went out some time in the morning. No one has seen him since then, no one knows where he went. We've been trying to trace him, but we can't find him anywhere.'

Vidya sank into a chair as if her legs had given way. 'But why? I mean, I don't understand. Why is everyone here?'

'This is Prem's doing, isn't it, love?' Cynthia's deep voice forestalled all of us. 'You're scared, aren't you, Prem, that what happened to Tony and Guru has happened to the Dean too?'

'Yes,' Prem said simply.

It was Rani who gave a kind of choked gasp and said in a muffled voice, 'You mean you think Ram is. . . .?'

Neeta sprang up from her chair and put her arms round Rani. 'Nonsense! No one thinks such a thing. Don't let them scare you, Rani.'

But Neeta was scared herself, she could scarcely hide her own fear.

'Why do we try to fool ourselves? Why don't we face the truth?' Cynthia's pose of lassitude had left her and her voice crackled with anger. 'My Tony was killed. I know it, we all know it. Whom are we trying to fool? One of us did it. Which one, Prem? Which one?'

Prem held Cynthia's hand and patted it gently. 'Take it easy, Cynthia. Take it easy,' he said soothingly.

'Easy? When Tony was killed! God, how can you say such a thing, Prem?'

'Killed? Tony?' Dr Shah's face glistened with sweat. 'Have you gone crazy?'

'No, no, not Tony, too. Not Tony, too,' Neeta stammered, her chin quivering.

'Yes, Tony. And before him, Guru. And, even before that, Prabhakar Tambe.' Prem gave Shyam a level look as he said this.

'You were part of that business yourself, Prem,' Shyam retorted.

'I know.' Prem had obviously decided there would be no more denials, no more lies.

'Rubbish!' Dr Kulkarni exploded, 'Guru had cancer and he died of it. And Tony was drunk. He fell into the temple tank in a drunken state and died.'

'Tony was not drunk. Don't forget, I've seen the post-mortem report. There was no trace of alcohol in his blood. He had bruises on his forehead and his fingertips were smashed. There were definite indications of his having been pushed into the tank. Can anyone explain that?' Prem asked softly. 'And Guru had enough pethidine in him to kill two men. Can you explain that, Dr Kulkarni?'

I knew Prem was bluffing, at least, about Guru. But his words had the desired effect. There was a stunned silence, followed by a harsh sound. It was Vimala laughing. There was something grotesque, obscene, about her laughter. As we stared at her in horrified amazement, the laughter imperceptibly changed into loud, harsh sobs. She buried her face in her lap. Her husband put an arm protectively around her and glared at the rest of us.

And then, at that moment, as if he had timed it, the Dean walked in. He looked exhausted, like a man who has run a marathon. For a moment, there was silence. I thought later of how unsurprised the Dean seemed to see so many of us in his house. Was it because he was so absorbed in what was going on in his mind? Or because he knew that this was going to happen? Whatever it was, when the exclamations and questions began, the Dean, leaning against the door, held one hand up, palm facing us. To stop all questions? All talk? Whatever it was, it worked. Words, questions ceased. And in the silence that followed, the Dean spoke, his voice husky, as if he hadn't used it for a long time.

'I have been to meet the Sethji,' he said.

Nobody spoke. There was absolute silence.

'I've resigned,' the Dean went on.

Still silence. At last, Vidya spoke. 'But, Ram, why?' It came out as a whisper. The Dean looked steadily at her as if wondering what to say. There had never seemed to be much resemblance between the two of them, but now their faces looked curiously alike. And when, finally, the Dean spoke, it seemed he was speaking, not to her, but to someone else. To himself? To Guru?

'One wrong,' he said, speaking softly—and so absolute was the silence that we all heard him clearly, 'one wrong breeds so many more. How long can I let it continue? Guru. Tony. How many more?'

Someone in the room seemed to be holding his (her?) breath in fear; the fear in the room was almost palpable.

The Dean didn't go on. It was Cynthia who prompted him. 'Yes, Guru,' she said, 'and Tony. But who did these things?'

'I don't know,' the Dean said simply. And now the fear in the room dissolved. There was only relief. 'Not yet.' Dr Shah got up and moved towards the Dean, his eyes fixed on the Dean's face in a pleading kind of way. 'But Dr Agarwal. . .'

'Later.' The Dean straightened himself and came to the centre of the room. 'Tomorrow, maybe.'

'But. . .' the man still persisted. His Adam's apple moved up and down as he swallowed. Vimala watched him with the same painful intensity with which he looked at the Dean.

'No,' the Dean said curtly. For the first time since I knew him, his gentle courtesy had deserted him. 'Not now. Keep it, whatever it is, for tomorrow.' Seeing Dr Shah's stricken face, the Dean spoke more gently. 'I'm sorry, but I'm too tired now. And I must apologize, too, it seems, for having worried all of you. Rani. . .?'

He turned to her, questioningly, for the first time since he had come into the room. As if his look had released her from something, she got up slowly from the sofa. She went to him and said, 'You've come back?' It was more a question than a statement. 'You've come back.' Now it was a statement. 'I thought you wouldn't.'

He smiled at her, the smile of an adult to a child. Comforting, reassuring. Rani responded to it instantly. The distrait stranger of the last few hours had disappeared. This was Rani once again.

'And where would I go? You know I will always come back to you. Come, Rani, time for bed. Goodnight, everyone.'

It was a very definite dismissal. And it was not to be questioned. We got up and walked out.

'The animals walked out two by two'—the words came into my mind from somewhere when I saw how couples huddled together, staying apart from the others. But I was alone. Where was Prem? I had presumed he had come out too when the rest of us walked out. But no, there he was, still in the hall, talking to the Dean. I could see Rani going upstairs, climbing slowly, wearily planting both her feet on a step before going on to the next, like a tired child. Vidya was just disappearing beyond the swing doors that led to the kitchen and the dining room. I sat down on the chair near the phone and waited for Prem. I couldn't hear what they were saying, they spoke in such low voices. I yawned again and again, my jaws finally aching with the repeated yawns.

At last they were done. The Dean moved towards the stairs. Prem came to me and I hoisted myself out of the chair. We went out and Prem banged the door behind us. It was a dark night. There was no rain, only a threat of it. The thunder was distant, muted, though each time it sounded closer.

'I should have brought the car,' Prem muttered. 'We must get home before the rain starts. I don't want you to get wet. Do you think you can walk a little faster?'

He put his arm round me, but I was so heavy and slow, he soon ceased to urge me on. We were on the road when a car stopped near us. It was Gautam.

'Come on, Manju, I'll drop you home. Get in, Prem.'

'Thanks, Gautam,' Prem said and held the door open for me, but I hesitated. 'Your baby and you can have the entire back seat to yourselves,' Gautam urged me. 'Get in.'

'I prefer to walk. Getting in and out of the car will take me more time than walking home.'

Both the men laughed and Prem closed the door. 'She's right, Gautam. But thanks, anyway.'

Gautam drove away with a wave of his hand and I wondered

whether he was truly unaffected by what was happening, or whether it was a pose. Or perhaps it was the insouciance of innocence. Innocence—was I always going to think of people now in terms of innocent or guilty? No, better to know the truth, whatever it is, whoever the guilty person may be.

When we got home, Prem said, 'Thank God, we're home. Go to bed, Manju, I'll get you a glass of milk. Should help you to sleep.'

But it didn't. I had a bad night. It was a physical restlessness—my limbs seemed to be incapable of being still—each position became uncomfortable after a few moments, so that I had to change into yet another position. Trying to turn sides was such a huge effort, I wondered how Nature could have made child-bearing such a clumsy process. Couldn't there have been a simpler way? Like birds, for example? The baby popping out of an egg instead of from inside the woman's body? I laughed at my fancy, but even that hurt. Thank God Prem was fast asleep. In a while, however, I had to wake him up. The uneasiness and discomfort had turned to twinges of pain.

'Prem,' I said softly. Then again, 'Prem.'

He woke up instantly and involuntarily reached for his glasses as he sat up. 'Manju, what is it? Have the pains begun?'

'I am not sure. I'm just very uncomfortable.'

'Go and empty your bladder and then we'll see.'

But in a while the pains ceased. 'Your baby has decided it's not yet time to leave the security of your womb and enter the world,' Prem said, laughing.

'Security? Poor thing. Must be restless and impatient to get out. Imagine being imprisoned in that tiny space for so long,' I said.

'Prisoner, eh? That's a new idea. But what a loving jailor! Anyway, try to sleep.'

Fortunately I did. But Prem obviously did not. He looked tired when he brought me a cup of tea in the morning. He was reluctant to leave me and go to work, but I persuaded him to go. 'Kamala is with me,' I said. 'And if I scream, I'm sure you'll be able to hear me wherever you are.'

I was not putting up a front. I felt distant and detached from all the ugliness that had come into our lives. 'Neeta's mother will be at home,' Prem suggested. 'Why don't you ask her to come home and stay with you until I return?'

But I didn't want anyone. After breakfast, Kamala and I pulled out Sonu's old baby clothes. I'd left them untouched until now, giving in to the superstitious fears my mother had instilled into me, that one should not make any preparations for a baby. My mother would be coming to us as soon as the baby was born. 'I'll get some clothes at the time,' she had said.

But Kamala and I decided to wash some of the old clothes. 'I'll iron them and have them ready before you come home,' she said. And like I had felt when Sonu was born, it seemed so strange, almost a miracle, that I would come back from the hospital with a new, living human being. Before taking the clothes away for washing, Kamala asked me, a little hesitantly, whether I wanted someone else to help with the housework. If I did, she said, she had an uncle's daughter who was willing to come.

'Yes, we'll need someone, there will be so much more work with a baby at home. And you'll have enough to do with Sonu and the baby. Ask your uncle's daughter to come and see me,' I told Kamala and felt more cheerful than I had for days. It felt good to be caught up in the most primeval act of giving birth; nothing else mattered. But the dark cloud came back with Prem. He came early, taking both Kamala and me by surprise. 'Lunch isn't ready,' I told him.

'I haven't come for lunch. I've come to talk to you.'

I had stayed cocooned in my home all morning and knew nothing of what was happening outside. But Prem told me that the hospital was abuzz with rumours that the Dean had resigned and that he would be leaving soon. Actually, Prem told me, the Dean had wanted to go away almost immediately. He was adamant, but had finally acceded to the Sethji's request to stay on until they found someone suitable to take his place. But he had made it a condition that they look for a temporary replacement and relieve him as soon as possible.

'The Dean came to see me in the lab. He said he wanted to talk to me in private.' And he made a proposal that staggered Prem. He wanted Prem to take on the Dean's post until the management found someone suitable.

'I told him I can't. For one thing, I don't have the necessary years of experience. No administrative experience, either. The Dean just waved away these objections. He said it would be for a short time only, he said he was sure I could manage. But when I told him how much resentment and bad feelings would result from putting me in his place, even if only for a short while, he hesitated. Finally he accepted my objection. Then I asked him, Why me?'

The Dean hesitated, Prem said, he found it hard to answer the question. Finally, he said it was because Prem was the one man he didn't have any doubts about. 'I reminded him it was I who had falsified Tambe's post-mortem report.'

'You did it because I told you to,' the Dean replied. He said that he would take full responsibility for what had happened, that he would absolve Prem of all guilt.

And then, Prem told me, the Dean had added, 'The buck stops with me. Didn't some American president say that? I vaguely remember reading somewhere that he had a notice on his table with these words. That's how it should be. If you're the boss, you have to take full responsibility for everything that happens—good or bad.'

Prem stopped there and I thought he had no more to tell me, but he went on. 'There's one more thing the Dean said which I must to tell you. He said I was the only one he could trust, because, he said, he knew Manju would never have married a dishonest man.'

He put his hand on mine and smiled at me. I felt close to tears, but I quelled them and asked Prem, 'But you did say no finally?'

'Of course. I'm not qualified to fill the position even temporarily. And I don't want the ugliness that will come with being in the Dean's chair. Even if I'm there only for a day, those feelings will remain.'

'Prem, why doesn't he suggest Vidya's name?'

'I asked him the same question. He said that the Sethji himself had suggested her name. But the Dean told me he had his doubts. She's not good at administration, he said, and not very good with people. You need that quality to be the boss, he said.'

Once again I thought of Guru saying, Skill is not enough. You need to be a good human being.

Prem suddenly looked at the time. 'Damn, it's late, I have to go back. If lunch is ready, I'll just have a bite before leaving.'

After lunch I fell asleep. And slept so long that when I woke up, the room was dark and the lights were on outside. I felt completely disoriented.

'You've had a long sleep, tai,' Kamala said, when I came out of my room.

'I'm feeling good, Kamala,' I said to her. I said the same to Prem as well when he came home. As if the Great Power which rules our lives had heard me and chuckled at the stupidity of stupid humans, by dinner time, all this sense of well-being had vanished. I could scarcely eat. Prem watched me anxiously and asked me, 'Would you like to lie down?'

'No, I'd rather try to walk a little.'

But soon pretence was no longer possible. I could not fool myself; the pains had begun. Prem went in and I heard him speaking to Kamala and then to someone else, Gautam, I guessed, on the phone. We had long prepared for this moment and it was a relief that things were being set in motion. Kamala came to me with a small bowl of curd. 'Eat this, tai,' she said and I remembered my mother doing the same thing before Sonu was born.

'Listen, Kamala,' I said, giving her back the bowl, 'you better go to Meeratai's house, don't stay alone at home.'

'You don't worry about me. Somebody should be in the house.'

Prem came to me and said, 'I can't get Gautam. The staff doesn't know where he is. I rang Vidya up and she says she'll come. In fact, she said, she'll pick us up and take us to the hospital.'

I nodded. I didn't have to take any decisions, I was no longer responsible for anything, not even for myself. Now it was only my baby and me.

Vidya came very promptly. Kamala accompanied me to the car and after helping me in, she said, 'Come back with a beautiful baby, tai.'

I had tears in my eyes. What was happening to me? I was becoming a ball of mushiness. 'Yes, I will, Kamala. And don't stay alone in the house. Go to Meeratai's house.'

'Come on, Manju, the sooner we get you to the hospital, the better for you. Comfortable there? All the room is for you and your baby,' she said, echoing Gautam's words. 'We'll be in the hospital in a few moments.'

But instead of taking the road to the hospital, Vidya drove along the road which led to the nurses' quarters.

'Why this way, Vidya?'

'I have to pick up Sister Nirmala. I like her to assist me, she's the best among them.'

The pain hit me, fiercer now, and washed over me like a great wave. When it receded, reluctantly, it seemed, leaving me sweating and limp, I heard Prem saying, 'But Vidya, we've gone past the nurses' quarters. Where are you going?'

I noticed that we were going through one of the side gates and were on the small road that led to the next village.

'Vidya, stop, you're going away from the hospital! Vidya, what are you doing, Vidya please stop. . .'

'No, Prem, I won't stop until you promise me. . .'

'Promise you what? What's going on?' I felt the car swerve when Prem suddenly grabbed the steering wheel.

'Don't do that. All right, I'll stop.'

The car stopped with a jerk, an abrupt jerk that made my head bang against the front seat with a thump, leaving me dizzy for a moment.

'Vidya, we have to go to the hospital. Manju is in labour. . .' I saw his hand move to the ignition key.

'I know that. That's why I am. . .' She removed the ignition key and held it in her hand.

'Vidya, Vidya, what's happened to you? Why are you doing this?'

'Don't pretend you don't know. It's you who's been egging

Ram to resign, isn't it? You want to become the Dean yourself, don't you? Ram told me he asked you to take charge temporarily. You! You're not fit to sit in his chair, Prem, you're not fit to clean his shoes. . .'

'Are you crazy, Vidya? What's that got to do with taking Manju to the hospital? Come on, Vidya, let's get there, let's admit Manju and then you and I can talk. If you don't want to drive, I will. Give me the keys.'

He lunged forwards and this time she drew back with a swift movement and said, 'Stop these stunts. This won't help you. Or Manju. I know your game now.'

'Don't be silly, Vidya. Why would I want to become the Dean?'

'Ambition.'

'My ambitions don't lie that way. And I'm totally unqualified for that job. Didn't the Dean tell you I refused?'

'That's just pretence. I know you, Prem. Now I have you in my power, I won't let you or Manju go until you give it to me in writing that you don't want the job. And that you'll make Ram take back his resignation.'

'How can I do that? I don't have any right to tell the Dean what he should do.'

The two of them were so engrossed in their battle that they ignored me, though I knew that Prem was fighting for me and for our child. I could feel him willing me to be quiet, not to let my presence obtrude on Vidya's consciousness. It was getting hard for me to sit up, sharp pains were stabbing my lower back, and the spasms getting worse; it was difficult to control my moans. I didn't know how long I could go on, I was not sure what would happen if Vidya's attention was drawn to me, I was frightened of what Prem would do if she tried to hurt me.

'You've spoilt everything. Guru first and then, you. God, how I hated that man.'

Hated Guru? The words hung between us in the cramped space of the car and I knew, as I was sure Prem did too, that she had killed Guru. She realized our comprehension almost immediately, but Prem, when he spoke, did so in an almost conversational tone, deflecting her thoughts, 'Why, Vidya, why did you hate him?'

'He was influencing Ram. What right did he have. . .?'

A small moan escaped me. I was losing control, the pain was getting the better of me.

'Vidya, let's go to the hospital. I'll admit Manju and then we can talk. I'll do whatever you want, I promise you that.'

His desperation reached her. When she spoke, her voice was cool. 'Too late, Prem. I can't let you go now, neither you, nor Manju.'

'Vidya, leave Manju out of this. She knows nothing. I've told you I'll go with you wherever you want, I'll do what you want. . .'

'No. I told you it's too late. Get out of the car—no, not you Prem. Manju, you get out. Come on, be quick.'

And now it penetrated through the haze that surrounded me—Vidya wanted to kill me, Vidya was going to kill me. Sonu, I thought desperately, my Sonu. . .

Vidya was waiting, holding the car door wide open for me. I sensed that Prem must have made some move, because she said, 'Prem, don't move. See this?' I saw a knife in her hand, a surgical knife. 'I won't hesitate to use this on Manju. Stay where you are, Prem. Come on, Manju, hurry up. Get out, get out fast.'

Get out fast? How could I? She was tugging at me, but it was not just my bulk that prevented me from getting out. It was the pain building up inside me, holding me now in a fierce grip, a pain that made everything else recede. Oh God, help me God. I could vaguely hear voices, I could feel Vidya still pulling me savagely. Suddenly I was out of the door and now the pain filled me until there was nothing but pain. As it reached a crescendo, I shrieked out my agony to the world. I could hear my own shriek coming back to me—again and again and again. Then I blacked out, I knew no more.

Fifteen

You go to sleep and dream and when you wake up, the dream
has gone. Nothing remains. But nightmares are not like that,
they will not let you be. Even if you can't remember the details
when you wake up, the fear remains, it hovers around you like
a dark cloud. And some nightmares lie dormant within you for
years, emerging at least-expected moments, releasing terrors
you thought were forgotten. So it is with us. It is all over, we
tell ourselves; life, we say, can now go back to normal, we can
put all that happened in those dreadful months behind us. It
was a nightmare that should be forgotten. But I know this can
never be; we can never forget or entirely shake off that time.
There is no escape from the knowledge; we look at one
another and the knowledge of what happened lies between
us. So does the sorrow and shame of the happenings. There is
not one of us who can say—I had nothing to do with it. But no
one talks of these things; they remain unsaid. We have created
a conspiracy of silence between us.

Prem and I spoke of it once, but only once, after I returned
home from the hospital. It was one afternoon, when the baby
was sleeping and Sonu was with my mother, that Prem told me
about the night our baby was born. 'Do you remember you
screamed just before you passed out?' he asked me. I did. I

knew nothing of what happened after I got out of the car, but I remembered that final scream. Later, it seemed to me that I had cried out to the world, to whatever power there is, to protect my baby. I didn't say this to Prem. Doctors, most doctors, and Prem certainly, are uncomfortable with the fanciful; they prefer facts, they believe only in what they perceive.

'Everything changed after that,' Prem went on. Vidya, he said, stood still as a statue for a moment when I slumped at her feet. Then she said to Prem, 'Help me, Prem.' She gave him the knife to hold and bent down to examine me. When they carried me to the grassy verge by the road, Vidya said, 'There's a coat of mine in the car, get it.'

She put the coat under me and, as coolly and competently as if she was in the fully-equipped labour room of the hospital, she set to her task of bringing my baby into this world. Prem thinks that my cry of pain, the final cry of a woman giving birth, suddenly brought out the trained obstetrician in her. I myself think that it was the miracle of birth, of life, that brought her back to her normal self. Whatever it was, she did what she had to do with professional competence. Prem told me that she used the knife with which she had threatened to kill me to cut the cord. Then she told Prem, 'Give me the baby and carry Manju back into the car'. Prem sat in the front seat holding our daughter—yes, she was a girl—in his arms, while Vidya drove us to the hospital. She walked into the hospital in her bloodied clothes—clothes smeared with my blood—sent out the nurses and a stretcher, then rang up Gautam and Cynthia and went back home.

None of us will ever know what went on between the three people in the house that night. Or, maybe it was just between the two of them, Rani staying out of it as always. Whatever they said—or didn't say—the next day a police van came to the Dean's house and took Vidya away. That it was Vidya who gave herself up is something neither Prem nor I doubt. We heard later that the Dean and Rani hired the best criminal lawyer in Bombay for Vidya. They also say that there is no real evidence against Vidya and that she may get off. But it is also possible that Vidya herself will admit to her guilt; both Prem and I think she will.

'Why did she do it, Prem? Why?' I asked him when he came to the end of his narrative.

He shrugged and said, 'We will never know the whole truth.'

In today's world, it is impossible for people not to whisper nasty things about the relationship between the Dean and his sister. But we who know the Dean leave the topic alone; muck-raking is not for us. Yes, Vidya's feelings for her brother were exaggerated, but that there could be something physical in that relationship. . .! No, it's impossible to believe. And what good does it do to bring up the muck now? One thing we know for sure is that Vidya greatly admired her brother, that he had been her idol since their childhood. It was he who had encouraged and helped her to become a doctor, something which their family, a conservative one, was totally against. It is also possible that she could not bear anyone being close to her brother, possible, too, that she was the one who distanced Rani from her husband. The truth is that we don't know much, we can only guess at most things. But one thing is certain, that she was jealous of Guru's influence over her brother. She was afraid that the Dean would follow Guru's advice and lose his position and reputation, both of which she held very dear. We guess that the Dean had told her about his plans of leaving and that she came that evening to Ashok's house prepared to kill Guru. It was easy for her to give him an injection; like Prem had said, Guru would think it normal for any of the doctors to give him an injection. It is also possible that she heard Tony boasting about what he knew and that she gave him a drink spiked with some drug, then pushed him into the tank and held his head under the water. But these, as I said, are mere surmise. We will never know the entire truth; we can never know the dark secrets of a human heart.

Cynthia tells me that the Dean wept before her. He begged for her forgiveness. 'Who am I to forgive him, Manju?' Cynthia asked me. And her eyes, as she said that, were bleak and I knew she was thinking of Tony and their life together. 'He's been punished enough, the poor guy.'

As she left, she voiced the thought that was in all of us— 'Why did she do it, Manju? Why? I will never understand it.'

None of us ever will. I have given up trying to make sense of what happened. But I cannot ignore the fact that two people died untimely deaths because of Vidya; nothing can wipe out the tragedy of that. It is unforgivable. I get furious when I hear people say, 'Well, Guru would have died anyway and Tony had come to the end of things.' That doesn't make it right. Each human being has the right to live his or her full span of life. Guru's words often come back to me: *If I die today, you die tomorrow.* Actually that's a misquotation. (I have to admit that it gives me a mischievous pleasure to think of Guru misquoting.) I looked up the quotation and what Sir Thomas More really said was: *Then in good faith is there no more difference between your grace and me, but that I shall die today, and you tomorrow.* I wonder whether Guru knew about Thomas More's life, about how he became a martyr because he chose to listen to his conscience, rather than obey a tyrannical king. Did Guru want to emulate him? But martyrdom is no longer possible today, for neither God, nor the country, nor anything else, demands such total allegiance. And so Guru may have decided to wake up other people's consciences—with such disastrous results. Meddler, someone called Guru. Maybe that's the right word. But Guru's intentions were good, I am sure of that. And he was a good friend to me, I will never forget that either.

During the rare times when I think of these matters, our conversation in the Dean's house comes back to me. And I remember how some of us spoke of punishment. Guru, I remember, had said that a crime should not go unpunished, that a criminal should pay for the crimes he had committed. And what crime can be worse than murder? There's nothing more terrible than taking a human life; no one has the right to change another person's time of death. Yes, Guru was right, the criminal must be punished. But punishment can take different forms. Even if they manage to get Vidya off, for lawyers and money can do a great deal, I wonder whether she will be able to live with herself. Someone spoke of atonement, but is any kind of atonement enough for destroying a human life?

But certainly there are other mistakes one can atone for. I see it in Prem, who is a changed man. He has not gone back to what he was before the dark cloud came down upon us; I know he no longer thinks that his work defines him, he no longer feels that he has to prove himself only through his work. The Dean had told Prem that he had absolved them all of what they had done after Prabhakar Tambe's death. But I know

Prem has not absolved himself. He now knows the demons that made him agree to do what the Dean asked him to do, he is trying to fight those demons.

But life, as I said earlier, goes on as before. I wish I could say that we are all better persons than we were, that we have come out of the ordeal purified and cleansed, that we have learnt our lesson. But life is never so definite, we can never change so completely. We remain chained to our old selves, we continue to muddle along, coping with each day as it comes.

And yet, there are changes. Vimala is trying to come out of her shell, her children come out and play with the other children, sometimes they smile at us and greet us when we meet them. Gautam has drawn his cloak of reserve even more closely around him. Vidya, who was once so important a part of his department, is never mentioned; it is as if she was never there. Strange, but that's Gautam! Ashok seems to be the same, but I often see him shooting anxious looks at Meera. I wonder why, because Meera looks the way she always had. Though I, who know her so well, can see the effort she makes to look the same. Sometimes I get a feeling that she is, in fact, parodying her earlier self. Shyam is a little grimmer than before, a little more silent. Perhaps, a little less arrogant. Neeta, on the other hand, looks more contented. Neeta came to me and told me Shyam wasn't leaving.

'It's his own decision. I haven't said anything It's his fight. I can only stand by and give him help if he wants it. So far, he hasn't asked me. It's too much to expect Shyam to learn humility overnight. But one day, I hope he will come to me.'

And there's Mriga. Can you call a fifteen-year-old girl a friend? I do. Mriga—her very movements have changed, as if something that was constricting her has gone. She grew up in those few days. She rarely speaks of her father now, not even in anger. I feel sorry for Dr Kulkarni. I wonder if he will, one day, say to himself, sorrowfully, 'I had a daughter and I lost her'? It seems unlikely. With her mother, Mriga seems to be on better terms. She comes to me very often, Mriga does. She talks and laughs and plays with the children. Sonu is a great fan of hers, and even our little one follows her with her eyes when Mriga is with her, she smiles when Mriga calls out to her.

We have named her Karishma. Yes, she is a miracle; she saved our lives. Each time I look at her, I think of the miracle of her birth, I think of the miracle of life itself. Cosmic accident? How could I have been so stupid as to think of human life as a cosmic accident? It's a miracle, nothing less than a miracle.

CPSIA information can be obtained
at www.ICGtesting.com
Printed in the USA
BVHW031602170223
658734BV00020B/1273/J